SCHOLASTIC

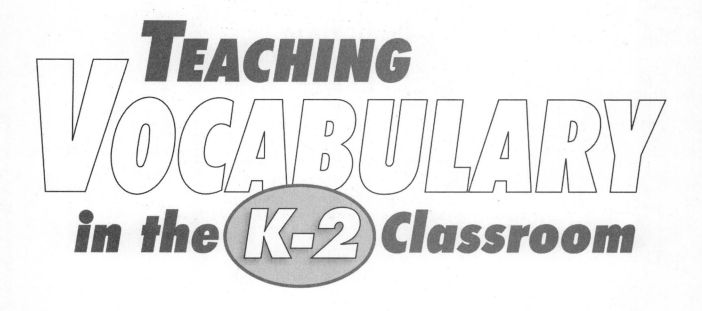

Teaching Vocabulary in the K-2 Classroom

Karen J. Kindle

Easy Strategies for Infusing Vocabulary Learning Into
Morning Meetings, Transitions, Centers, and More

New York • Toronto • London • Auckland • Sydney
Mexico City • New Delhi • Hong Kong • Buenos Aires

Teaching *Resources*

Dedication

To Peter,
who taught me to dream again

Many thanks to
Dr. Lee Mountain for her encouragement

Special thanks to
the children who have taught me as I have taught them.

Cover design by Jason Robinson
Cover photo by Ellen B. Senisi
Interior design by Sarah Morrow

Copyright © 2008 by Karen J. Kindle
All rights reserved. Published by Scholastic Inc.
Printed in the U.S.A.
ISBN-13: 978-0-439-02426-6
ISBN-10: 0-439-02426-9

1 2 3 4 5 6 7 8 9 10   40   14 13 12 11 10 09 08

Contents

CHAPTER 4 ✳ *Using Centers to Assess and Promote Language Development*

CHAPTER 5 ✳ *Weaving Vocabulary Into Literacy Activities*

To the Teacher

The idea of vocabulary infusion was born in a classroom—my classroom. Through many years of teaching, I noticed that one thing my struggling readers had in common was a vocabulary deficit. Some students were second-language learners. Some were economically disadvantaged. Some were currently in speech classes for language delays. But the common thread was language use that differed from the language of school and books.

I remembered how I had helped my own children learn language and build their vocabularies at home, and wondered if I could do some of the same things in the classroom. I started making vocabulary infusion activities a regular part of the daily school routine. I immersed my students in words.

My work grew and blossomed. My strategies multiplied. Vocabulary infusion became my way of life in communicating with my students, a way of life that I'd like to share with you. The infusion activities in this book are the ones I have used in my classrooms with my students over my eighteen years as a teacher.

Infusing vocabulary into your instruction is like making a cup of tea. The tea bag is immersed in the water. As it steeps, the flavor of the tea swirls around and around until the entire cup has been infused with flavor. Infusing your classroom with rich vocabulary works much the same way, surrounding children with language that extends and expands their world.

So put aside your lesson plans and papers for a moment. Sit back and enjoy a cup of tea. Consider the possibilities of infusion for your students.

Karen J. Kindle

CHAPTER 1

Vocabulary Infusion

A Process, Not a Program

At first glance, it may look like any other primary classroom. Children are busy at the task of learning to read and write. But look and listen a little closer. Look around the room and notice the rich written language. The walls are filled with unusual words written on charts, lists, and posters. Children refer to these lists as they work in the writing center incorporating unusual words into their compositions. Andy is writing in his journal. He stretches the word out and carefully writes what he hears. *Chre-bu-shay*. Andy is writing about a trebuchet, a medieval weapon similar to a catapult.

Listen. You hear *lots* of talking. Tommy implores the teacher not to step on a spider that is terrorizing the girls. "Don't kill it. It's a noun!" Two little girls are debating whether Mary's new dress is cornflower or sapphire blue.

This is the infusion classroom. It is an atmosphere filled with language that celebrates words and wordplay. What makes the infusion classroom different is intent. Vocabulary development becomes part of the fabric of the day instead of an isolated component. The result is a language-rich environment that fosters word learning each and every day.

Vocabulary Development: A Critical Need

The link between vocabulary and reading comprehension has been well established in reading research (Baumann, Kame'enui, & Ash, 2003). Vocabulary has been identified as one of the critical components of reading by the National Reading Panel (2000), and vocabulary size has been shown to be predictive of reading achievement (Biemiller, 2001). Some research is showing a relationship between vocabulary size, word identification, and phonemic awareness (Metsala, 1999). Additionally, lack of content vocabulary has been related to student failure on high-stakes testing (Chall & Snow, 1988).

Research has also shown us that our at-risk students are those who are most likely to start school with vocabulary deficits. Insufficient word knowledge has been identified as a key factor in the achievement gap that exists (Hirsch, 2005). We also know that insufficient word knowledge is strongly linked to the family's socioeconomic status (Hart & Risley, 1995).

The increasing diversity in our schools further complicates the issue. English language learners are present in most urban and suburban classrooms. These children may or may not be fluent in the language of their parents. Parents often try to speak only English at home in hopes of accelerating the language acquisition process. The unfortunate results of such good intentions may be children who speak very little of their home language, but are not fluent in English either. These children are at a severe disadvantage in school.

Why Balanced Literacy Isn't Enough

When I talk with teachers about the need for developing the vocabulary of our students, I see nods of agreement throughout the group. Teachers who work with students struggling with reading and writing have long known that vocabulary is a critical factor in students' lack of success. Sessions on vocabulary development at literacy conferences are numerous and well attended, as classroom teachers seek solutions to a very real problem. Despite our best efforts, some children are still lagging behind.

Like most teachers, I worked very hard to provide the best possible instruction to my students, carefully blending the components of early literacy into a balanced program. I incorporated phonemic awareness and phonics into my daily instruction and formed guided reading groups. I read aloud to my students and provided time for independent reading through a schoolwide sustained silent reading program.

Overall, my students were successful with their emergent and early readers, and I was proud of the progress they made. But as I talked with colleagues in the upper elementary grades, a disturbing pattern began to emerge. The children, with whom I had worked so hard, were again lagging behind their peers as they encountered the more rigorous texts of third grade and beyond. In talking to their teachers, I learned that in most cases, the problem was comprehension. They were able to decode the words, but they did not know what they meant. The problem was vocabulary.

Why wasn't the vocabulary problem apparent from the start? The answer, in part, may be found in the type of instruction that dominates classrooms today. Primary teachers work hard to help their students master the early literacy skills that research shows are essential to reading success. Phonemic awareness and phonics instruction have helped many children master the alphabetic principle, and yet the achievement gap persists. Biemiller and Boote (2006) suggest that current instructional methodologies assume that vocabulary will be built after the children become successful with decoding. Wide reading will then supply the vocabulary they need. Experience in the classroom, however, tells us that by then it will be too late. Substantial gaps exist in vocabulary size when children enter school (Hart & Risley, 1995). Studies show that these gaps continue to widen throughout elementary school (Biemiller, 2003; White, Graves, & Slater, 1990).

When our youngest readers are dealing with the early emergent texts, they are often successful. By necessity, books written for early readers have simple, repetitive language that is a fairly close match to the oral language structures used by the children. Decodable texts feature simple words and a controlled vocabulary to ensure student success. The concepts presented in the text are typically familiar and concrete. *I see a bird. I see a dog.* These early readers serve an important function in reading instruction, but do little to expand children's vocabularies. Texts of this kind are also supported with illustrations for students to confirm their ideas as they construct meaning. Even when the vocabulary presented is new, the concepts are familiar enough for the child to grasp the meaning.

Meaning, or comprehension itself, is quite limited in these early texts—simply reading the sentence gives you most of the meaning. Many of our at-risk kids experience relative success with the typical early reader due to its predictable text, controlled vocabulary, and supportive illustrations. Even rare and unusual words are easily learned and read with enough scaffolding. Many of the texts used in Reading Recovery™ were written by Joy Cowley, a native of New Zealand. One emergent reader introduces the reader to the giant weta, a large insect similar to a cockroach. The accompanying illustration supports the connection between the word and a familiar concept, and the weta presented little difficulty for my beginning readers.

Things become much more difficult as the reading level increases. Text becomes less patterned and the sentence structures become more complex. The student's oral language is no longer a scaffold to reading. The vocabulary used in the text is no longer part of the student's listening or speaking vocabulary, and comprehension suffers. Additionally, the vocabulary becomes more abstract. The concepts represented are no longer familiar to the student.

And so I began thinking about ways that I could support the development of vocabulary and expressive language in my students. How do we learn new words? How did my own children acquire their extensive vocabularies? Maybe that would provide some insight into how I could help my students. My questions eventually led to the development of *vocabulary infusion*, a strategy that has been successful in my classroom. The infusion concept is grounded in research on the ways that children learn new words.

A Look at Vocabulary Acquisition

Vocabulary instruction has often been equated with workbooks and dictionary drills. Lists of words are given on Monday, memorized for the Friday test, and never seen or heard again. We now know that this is not effective vocabulary instruction (Blachowicz & Fisher, 2000). Most words are learned incidentally as children encounter them in the language environment, rather than through formal instruction. Additionally, knowing a word means more than memorizing a definition. Words are learned gradually, through repeated exposures in meaningful contexts (Nagy & Scott, 2000). Infusion is based on the principles of gradual word learning and incidental word learning.

Levels of Word Knowledge

First we must consider what it means to know a word. Words can be known on various levels. We may say we know a word when we recognize it in print or in conversation, but our understanding of that term may be very limited. My son attends college in Galveston, Texas, on the Gulf of Mexico. Although busy surfing and fishing, he finds time to attend some classes, and recently mentioned something to me about the *neap tide*. I had heard the term before and knew that it was a type of tidal condition—but no more than that. My son was able to explain the neap tide in relation to the phases of the moon. He understood it on a far different level than I did. We both knew the word, but his understanding was much deeper than mine.

There are several models for levels of word knowledge posited by researchers (i.e., Dale, 1965; Graves, 1986; Nagy & Scott, 2000), but most include the following levels in some fashion:

1. Recognition

2. Use in limited contexts

3. Knowledge of alternate meanings and uses

4. Understanding how the word fits into the larger lexicon

As an example of how these levels might apply to our students' learning, consider the familiar word *angry*. Most of our students would recognize the word if they heard it in conversation and some might even recognize it in print. They have heard it before and understand something about the associated emotion. They may be able to associate it with the more childlike synonym mad and substitute it in a similar context: *My mom was angry at me*.

But most children would have difficulty when encountering the word in a figurative context: *The farmer saw the angry clouds and hurried to finish his work.* They lack knowledge of alternate meanings and uses for the word.

Last, how does the word fit into the lexicon? While many children would say that *mad* and *angry* would be synonyms, do the terms conjure up the same connotation for you as a mature language user? Or would you rank them in some type of hierarchy? Is there a degree of formality associated with *angry* that is not present with *mad*?

Clearly, what we mean by knowing a word is a complex concept. Deep word knowledge is built over time, by many exposures in varied contexts. Yet this is exactly the type of word knowledge that we want for our students.

Incidental Exposure and Immersion

Children learn new words at a staggering rate. Researchers suggest that young children learn an average of eight to ten new words *every day*, the majority of them through incidental exposure. This exposure may come from conversational exchanges with more proficient language users, from overhearing conversations, media, or from being read aloud to. Of course, some words are learned through direct instruction, but these are a minority considering the huge number of words the average child acquires each year. Learning vocabulary through incidental exposure led to the application of immersion, a pedagogical approach borrowed from the language acquisition literature (Genesee, 1985), which suggests that if we surround children with rich and varied language, they will build their vocabularies. Immersion does develop vocabulary and oral language (Cummins, 1983), but it is not sufficient to make up for the deficits in vocabulary size that some children have when they enter school. Early deficits in vocabulary only increase over time (Biemiller, 2001). We must find a way to help students overcome these difficulties; we must actively infuse words into their vocabulary.

Infusion: Research-Based Practice That Enhances Vocabulary Acquisition

Infusion takes the rich language environment recommended by immersion a step further. New words are introduced as part of a purposeful and planned process and not left to chance. The teacher looks for opportunities to embed the words of mature language users into every portion of the day, providing children with multiple opportunities to hear and use new and interesting words. Infusion is consistent with the principles of vocabulary instruction recommended by leading researchers in the field.

Principles of Vocabulary Instruction

The vocabulary activities in the infusion classroom are based on the principles of vocabulary instruction that research has identified as effective. In *The Vocabulary Book* (2006), Graves suggests that instruction should be based on four principles:

1. A rich and varied language experience
2. Instruction on individual words
3. Strategies for learning new words
4. Fostering word consciousness

Words are best learned when they are presented in multiple contexts, when students have frequent exposures over time in ways that develop depth of meaning, and when children are actively involved in the construction of meaning—that is, when they are engaged in activities that develop understanding by demonstrating the relationships and connections between words.

Vocabulary infusion is my answer to meeting a very real need. It provides my students with vocabulary instruction that is supported by research. And it really requires no materials per se; it is as simple as taking a teachable moment and infusing it with vocabulary. When you create an environment that values words, it is evident in the charts and lists of words on the walls of the classroom; it is evident in the children's writing; it is evident in the conversations you hear. It worked for my students, and I believe it will work for yours.

Getting Started With Infusion

Infusing vocabulary into my classroom did not happen overnight. It was a long, gradual process as I found more and more opportunities to incorporate vocabulary into my instruction.

It takes time to feel right. My young friend Jennifer decided she would try to use some vocabulary infusion ideas with her class while her students were in the cafeteria. When she commented to the children on what a *magnificent feast* they had for lunch that day, they looked at her as though she had lost her mind. Based on the lunch served at most schools, I might have, too! She was discouraged, interpreting the children's reaction to mean she had done something wrong.

But consider what had happened. First of all, the children noticed the new, unusual words she had used; they cannot learn the words if they don't notice you have used them. But it takes time for us as teachers to develop these routines so it feels natural when we talk this way to our students.

As a result of her continued efforts, rich vocabulary is regularly featured on the menu and an expected part of the lunchroom experience. Jennifer has even found that she actually enjoys lunch duty now!

Conclusion

In the chapters that follow, you will read about some of the infusion activities that I have used with my students. They are meant to guide and encourage you as you begin the process of vocabulary infusion in your classroom. The ideas and activities presented have been a work in progress for many years. Some of the suggestions require thoughtful planning, while others arise from the teachable moment. Infusion teaching requires creativity and a great deal of flexibility!

As you begin to try infusion strategies, select one portion of the day and start from there. Gradually, as you and your students become comfortable with the process, expand infusion to other parts of the day. Before long, you will discover opportunities to develop vocabulary from bell to bell.

And don't be surprised if you find that *your* vocabulary increases as well! Infusion teaching will heighten your own awareness of language and send you rushing to the thesaurus to find new ways to satisfy your students' newfound hunger for WORDS.

> **A word is dead**
>
> A word is dead
> When it is said,
> Some say.
>
> I say it just
> Begins to live
> That day.
>
> —*Emily Dickinson*

CHAPTER 2

Oral Language Development

My young neighbor will be ready to read when she gets to school. She often greets me as I return home at the end of the day. "Dad, our neighbor is home," she will call to her father as he works in the garage. She chatters about the latest happenings at her preschool and the newest antics of her baby sister. She shows me the pictures she has colored and tells stories of her play. There seems little doubt that she has the language skills and vocabulary required to be successful in school—long before any formal reading instruction has occurred.

Many of our students are not as fortunate. Vocabulary deficits and language differences will challenge them as they seek to be successful in the school environment. These children need additional support to develop their oral language skills, the foundation on which reading and other academic skills will be built.

The Role of Oral Language

Most language arts programs for the primary grades include listening and speaking components in their design. We may assess these skills as mandated by district or state requirements, but we focus so long and hard on teaching reading and writing that there seems to be little time for anything else. When listening and speaking are included, they often seem to be activities that are added in as afterthoughts rather than as part of a systematic plan for language development. Yet, research tells us that oral language proficiency is strongly related to reading achievement (Nation & Snowling, 2004).

Receptive language and listening skills will impact how much children are able to benefit from instruction and gain vocabulary from the language around them. It just makes sense—if they don't listen, or can't understand you, the best-planned lesson will prove unproductive. In fact, listening comprehension is considered to be a broad measure of reading comprehension potential (McCormick, 2007).

Expressive language has an obvious link to writing. Young children's writing mirrors their patterns of speech in its sentence structures, word choices, and spelling. The child who can tell you a story is more likely to be able to write a story. The child who can describe something orally is more likely to be able to do so in writing as well. Instruction in oral language structure will support the development of your students' writing skills, as well as develop their expressive language.

The development of expressive and receptive language skills is vital to the success of any early literacy program. Prekindergarten and kindergarten teachers focus on these skills a great deal in their curricula, but when the emphasis shifts to learning to read, time for oral language instruction is hard to find. In order for these skills to continue to develop, teachers need to continue to focus on them in first and second grade as well.

Oral Language and the At-Risk Student

For many of our at-risk students, the language experiences of their preschool years do little to prepare them for literacy instruction. The way they have learned to use language is different from what they encounter in the classroom. These children need exposure, not just to vocabulary, but to the structures of language that will help them with comprehension and written expression.

Proficient readers make use of a variety of cueing systems to construct meaning as they read. Effective use of the syntactic cueing system depends on the match between the child's oral language and the language of the text. In Reading Recovery™, one of the prompts used when a child makes a structural miscue is, "Does that sound right?" With many of my students, the answer would be yes. The miscue does sound right to them because it reflects how they use language. For these children, the syntactic cueing system hinders rather than helps their reading.

Tests of English language proficiency point out the important role that syntax and vocabulary play in language acquisition. Students who are classified as limited English proficient are tested periodically to determine continued eligibility and service hours. In some cases, students who express themselves quite well in the course of daily classroom activity have difficulties due to the specific vocabulary requirements of test items. They may know many words—but not the specific words encountered on the test. In other cases a student may know the correct word but be unable to produce an answer to the question that is syntactically correct. For example, the child may respond to the question "What is this?" with a single-word answer of "flag"—he knows the word, but is unable to form a complete sentence—"It is a flag." Specific instructional needs may differ, but all children require further language development to become proficient readers and writers of English.

Developing Oral Language

In the context of the classroom, children learn language through conversation. Listening to the way the mature language user expresses his ideas provides children with a model. McGee and Richgels (2003) suggest that both the quantity and quality of teacher-child interactions are critical components of language development. The language that you use, both in formal instructional times and informal exchanges that occur throughout the day, exposes your students to new words and new sentence structures. It is a natural continuation of the way they learned language as infants and toddlers. As children make their first attempts to speak, their caregivers use the techniques of recasting, repetition, questioning, and elaboration to further develop the child's language. These same techniques can be effective in the classroom.

For example, if a student reports to the class, "I lost two tooths!" consider responding in a way that acknowledges his message, but extends his oral language. For example: "Wow! You lost two teeth." Recasting consists of rephrasing the child's language into more conventional language.

"Wow, I can see you lost two teeth. You lost your two front teeth." Repetition consists of rephrasing the child's remark, then repeating it with emphasis or slight elaboration.

"You lost two teeth. When did they fall out?" Questioning consists of recasting followed by a question to extend the conversation.

"Your teeth were loose and wiggly yesterday, and now they have fallen out." Elaboration consists of embedding the child's remark into a more complex structure. These simple techniques can enhance children's oral language development in a natural way.

Easy-to-Implement Strategies for Developing Oral Language

In addition to the techniques described in the previous section, I found three methods that always helped make a difference in developing students' oral language. I would ask students to "tell me in a sentence," to "tell me more about it," or I would ask them a question.

Tell Me in a Sentence

Most of the time, when you ask your students a question, they respond with a single word or phrase. Of course, we all do the same in normal conversation. But one of the easiest things you can do to support the language development of your students is to insist that they tell you in a sentence. They need to practice expressing themselves in complete sentences to develop the syntax they need to become successful readers and writers. Children who find this task difficult will also struggle when asked to write complete sentences in answer to questions.

This strategy can be used throughout the day. My students knew that it was coming. Even in the cafeteria, if a child raised his hand and I asked him what he needed, he knew that just saying "ketchup" wasn't going to work. Other students would prompt, "You have to say it in a sentence!"

The Art of Asking Questions

Part of getting students to answer questions in complete sentences depends on developing your ability to ask good questions. Good questions are those that can not be answered in a word. In the cafeteria example above, I learned that asking the child "May I help you?" led to answers in complete sentences, while a question like "What do you need?" was far more likely to elicit a one-word answer. Questions that begin with *how* and *why* result in more extensive answers than *who*, *what*, and *where* questions. Instead of asking a student, "Where did you go for spring vacation?" try asking, "How did you spend your spring break?" The first question can be answered in a word—*nowhere*, or *Disneyland*. The second will result in a sentence—"We went to the lake."

Not every question can be phrased in a way that requires elaboration, but we need to be on the lookout for those opportunities and ask those questions whenever possible. Elaboration serves to extend the conversation, and the more you talk with your students, the more opportunities they have to benefit from your use of language.

Tell Me About It

Young children love to tell you their stories. They can't wait to tell you what happened over the weekend or to show you their newest treasure. You can take advantage of their natural desire to talk to you and develop their oral language by simply asking, "Can you tell me more about that?" This simple response encourages children to extend their thinking, adding details and elaboration. The ability to tell their story leads into writing personal narratives. As a child tells you her story, ask for clarification.

- "What happened next?"
- "Who was with you?"
- "Where did this happen? I am trying to get a picture in my mind of what that looked like."
- "Can you tell me more about . . . ?"

Through your prompts and questions, you can let the child know what elements are needed for a good story.

McGee and Richgels (2003) recommend that you model the process by sharing your own experiences with the children. They love to hear stories about you and your family. As you relate your tale, include rich vocabulary and interesting details. Your students will begin to model their storytelling after your example.

Oral Language Activities

How do classroom teachers incorporate oral language instruction into their already jam-packed days? Apply the infusion concept! Opportunities for the development of oral language are present throughout the day. The activities that follow can be incorporated into any circle time or group gathering in your daily routine. Most of the activities can be done orally for prereaders and adapted to include text as children develop word recognition and identification skills.

Wordplay

Wordplay develops children's interest in and awareness of words. Children seem to have a natural affinity for the rhythm and rhyme of language, but they also need to develop conscious attention to words so they can pick unfamiliar vocabulary out of the stream of language around them. Wordplay can come in the form of games, puzzles and riddles, or just in the flow of conversation.

A conversation with my young nephew illustrates the type of exchange that can foster word awareness in a natural and fun way. When his sister was an infant, I had given her a stuffed bunny that became her constant companion. Through much love, it had become tattered and worn and was affectionately known as Hole Bunny. Recently, my nephew and I were looking at family photos and we came across a picture that included Hole Bunny in her original state. I commented, "There is Hole Bunny when she was Whole Bunny with a *w*." At first, he looked at me with a puzzled expression—then he got the joke and, as children will do, repeated it to everyone in the family. When my nephew reads *The King Who Rained*, or *Chocolate Moose for Dinner*, he will be primed to get the humor. Natural exchanges of this kind do not take planning or materials—just a teacher who looks for opportunities to seize the teachable moment.

Wordplay on the Internet

The Internet is an amazing resource for wordplay. I regularly receive e-mails that involve plays on words. While much of it is inappropriate for children, you can come across some excellent examples.

- When a clock is hungry, it goes back for seconds.

- A calendar's days are numbered.

- A bicycle can't stand alone: it is too tired.

Getting the joke requires understanding alternate meanings for these common words. This depth of word knowledge is a hallmark of a well-developed vocabulary.

Word Games

Word games, such as riddles and hink pinks, provide opportunities for children to develop high-order thinking skills such as making inferences and drawing conclusions (Buchoff, 1996).

Hink pinks are rhymed word pairs that answer a riddle. They are classified according to the number of syllables in the answers. For example, hink pinks are one-syllable answers, hinky pinkys are two-syllable responses, and hinkety pinketys have three. These may be difficult for children at first, so start with very simple ones.

- What do you call an overweight pet? *A fat cat*

- What do you call an angry father? *A mad dad*

As the students develop their vocabularies and understand the concept, you can make the clues more difficult; an *obese feline* would be a more difficult clue. Target vocabulary can be incorporated into the clues.

Examples of hink pinks are not hard to find. An Internet search yielded over three thousand hits for hink pinks, including many sites developed by teachers and their students that will be especially appealing to your class. Our local newspaper has a feature on the puzzle page each day called Wordy Gurdy, which operates on the same principle. While geared for adults, some of the examples can be adapted for use with your students. With a little practice, your students will be writing their own hink pinks!

- What do you call a chubby kitty? *A fat cat*

- What do you call a huge hog? *A big pig*

- What do you call a rabbit that tells jokes? *A funny bunny*
- What is a cute young cat? *A pretty kitty*
- What do you call a crying father? *A sad dad*

Hangman

My children called this game Wheel of Fortune, after the popular TV program, but it is simply a "kinder, gentler" version of Hangman. This activity can be done on the chalkboard for whole-group involvement, but I discovered that for small groups and circle times, using a cookie sheet and magnetic letters works even better. This format offers great advantages for young learners by allowing them to take the role of the moderator.

1. The moderator (or teacher) selects a word for play. The word may come from any chart or list in the room, or the student may pull a card from a word box that you use to collect vocabulary words that have been taught. The moderator may also suggest a word collected from home.

2. Using a dry-erase marker, make the appropriate number of blanks in the center of the cookie sheet. This lets the students know how many letters are in the word.

3. On the side facing the moderator, use magnetic letters to spell out the word. This way the moderator does not have to remember the letters that have been called or how to spell the word—it is right there for him.

4. Students take turns suggesting letters to form the word. They must ask in the form of a question, "Is there a B?" or "Are there any As?" The moderator responds with "Yes, there is a B," or "No, there are no Bs." Clues can be given as to the word's meaning if appropriate. Additionally, you can require the team that guesses the word to use it correctly in a sentence.

Sentence Hangman

In this version, sentence structure is the focus and students learn to develop their use of the syntactic cueing system to predict what words would make sense (Hall, 1995). For young children, begin with a simple sentence related to something that occurred during the course of the day or a unit of study. For example:

On Friday we are going on a field trip to the zoo.

Write the number of blanks on the board and supply a key word to give the children a clue about the schema for the sentence. In this example, you might reveal "Friday" to clue the children in on the time of the event. You may need to support the children at first by providing the first letter of a few words, but as they develop their skills, this won't be needed. Hall (1995) provides a scoring system that works well for older students, but for younger kids, I find it detracts from the focus of the game. When students supply the correct words, a quick "How did you know?" supports verbalization of strategies and supports the understanding of all of the students.

Cooking

Concerns about allergies, health, and safety have made cooking in the classroom difficult to do, but if it is possible to do some cooking with your students, it is well worth the effort. Cooking with young children provides tremendous opportunities for vocabulary development. Words such as *mix, stir, beat, blend,* and *whip* can be demonstrated in authentic contexts. Science concepts and terms such as *liquid* and *solid* can be easily demonstrated as pudding or Jell-O is made. Measuring ingredients provides rich opportunities for math concepts to be explored.

- "Which holds more: a tablespoon or a ¼ cup?"
- "Let's add a pinch of salt to the soup."

Even the utensils used in cooking represent a wealth of vocabulary as you ladle the soup, use the spatula to flip the pancakes, or use the tongs to turn the hot dogs.

Crayon Box

Sometimes we have only to look in our classrooms to find sources of rich vocabulary and language for our students. I used to dread the giant boxes of crayons that some students arrived with on the first day of school. The box was too big to fit in the desks and it just seemed to cause confusion. An activity as simple as coloring the United States flag resulted in questions and disagreements.

- "Which color of red do I use?"
- "Is this blue OK for the flag?"

The sight of American flags colored with cornflower blue and red-violet made me wish I had insisted that all my students had the small eight-packs with basic colors!

Then I realized the possibilities for new words contained in that giant box. In Crayola's™ box of 48 crayons, you can find olive, salmon, sea green, tan, spring green, melon, lavender, mahogany, macaroni and cheese, purple mountain's majesty, chestnut, tumbleweed, green yellow, sepia, timberwolf, cadet blue, peach, raw sienna, goldenrod, granny smith apple, black, burnt sienna, wisteria, cerulean, apricot, yellow, green, white, orange, yellow orange, violet, dandelion, gray, violet red, brown, blue, yellow green, red violet, cornflower, scarlet, indigo, sky blue, red orange, blue violet, red, blue green, and carnation pink.

Imagine the possibilities of the mega 64-color box of crayons!

Crayon Activities

1. **Find a color:** Select a color from the box. Ask students to identify a color that is lighter, darker, or similar to the target color.

   - Find a color that is lighter than cadet blue.

   - Find a color that is similar to timberwolf.

2. **Comparing colors:** Select two colors from the box that have similar names. For example, you might choose red orange, orange red, orange, and red. How does the word order reflect the amount of each color in the name?

3. **Cafeteria connection:** Take the discussion to the cafeteria. Which color green would be closest to celery? Carrots? Your chocolate ice cream?

4. **Making connections:** Many of the color names represent animals, flowers, or other items. Show your students a picture of a timber wolf and discuss the color gray in the box. Why is timberwolf a good name for this color? Other examples might include wisteria, carnation, olive, salmon, apricot, or peach. Discussions of this kind lead naturally into the use of similes and metaphors.

5. **Name that color:** After your students have discovered how the color names are developed, they can generate their own names for colors. Provide them with paint chips obtained from your local hardware or discount store. Ask them to create names to go along with the colors by comparing them to pictures of animals, flowers, or birds. A brilliant blue might be named Blue Morpho after a student compares it to a picture of the butterfly of that name. This activity can later be placed in a center. Provide index cards or paper for the child to draw a picture of the plant or animal with the color crayon he is naming.

6. **What color was it?:** In the course of conversation, ask children to clarify when they use a color word. For example, as a student tells a story about a blue balloon he got at the zoo, ask if the blue was more like sky blue or indigo. Explain to your students that details like this help you to get a clearer picture in your mind. As we discussed earlier in this chapter, children are more likely to use these details in their writing if they use them in their telling.

Keyword Connections

This strategy is more appropriate for use with children who are already reading, but with a few adaptations, it also can be used to develop oral vocabulary. Research supports the use of visualization as a strategy for learning unfamiliar words. Using an illustration to help children connect a word and its definition is an effective strategy that you can use in your classroom. For young children, this activity can be developed in a game-like format, using either pictures or objects. Select a word like *sprinkler*. Locate pictures or items that would be associated with the word and support comprehension. In this case you could hold up a container of sprinkles (the kind you put on ice cream) and some blades of grass. The sprinkles reinforce the concept of what it means to sprinkle, and the grass provides a clue as to the function of the word. To help children understand the word *nestle*, you might show them a picture of bird eggs in a nest. Variations of this activity include the following:

1. **Compound Words:** Compound words are frequently practiced this way. For example, *butter* + *fly* = *butterfly*, *sky* + *scraper* = *skyscraper*. Children enjoy making puzzle cards, flip books, and pop-up books in this format.

2. **Picture Puzzles:** Locate a picture that clearly depicts a target vocabulary word. Cut the picture into pieces to match the number of letters in the word. For example, the word *walrus* would be cut into six pieces. Students guess letters in the word, just like in Hangman, but as each letter is correctly guessed, a piece of the picture is revealed.

3. **Picture Sentence Puzzles:** Select a photograph or illustration that depicts an action. For example, you may use an illustration of Jack jumping over the candlestick from a book of Mother Goose rhymes. Generate a sentence that describes what is happening in the picture: *Jack leaps over the candlestick.* Play the Sentence Hangman game described earlier in this chapter, but reveal pieces of the picture as clues.

Picture This

Proficient readers notice details, ask questions, and draw conclusions as they construct meaning from text. Although we work hard to teach these skills in our classrooms, young children do this naturally as they study and learn from the world around them. By developing children's ability to think and talk about what they see, we are developing foundation-level skills for reading comprehension.

Recently, while waiting for a table at our local IHOP, I was seated by the front counter, which had been decorated with a jungle scene, complete with plastic wild animals. A young boy who looked to be about four years of age was crouched down, carefully studying the scene before him. "That's a jungle, right?" he asked his mother. He had noticed the variety of animals present in the scene and had drawn the conclusion that it was a jungle.

The scene had a terraced hillside with a rhino perched on top. This detail seemed to bother the boy, who asked, "Why is he on top?" What a great question! It took the mom by surprise, but after a moment of thought she responded, "So he can see everything." The boy went on attending to details, naming the various animals in the scene: the giraffe, the tiger (which he explained was hiding in the bushes), and the king (the lion). When he commented on the mother and baby lions, his mother corrected him, stating that they were cheetahs because they had spots.

Can we teach our students to engage the text in the same way as this young boy was engaged in constructing meaning from the counter display? We can't construct three-dimensional scenes, of course, but we can model this kind of process with photographs and illustrations.

1. Locate an interesting photograph from a book, newspaper, magazine, or the Internet. The picture needs to be large enough for the children to see clearly. A smaller picture can be used for a small-group activity; big book or Internet pictures that can be displayed on a large screen work best for whole-class activities.

2. Introduce the picture to the children. Ask them to tell you what they observe in the picture. Remember to have them tell you in a sentence.

3. Initial responses are likely to be simple observations, such as *I see a horse*. Through a series of questions, prompt your students to look deeper and more thoughtfully at the picture. What can we learn about horses from examining this picture? How is a horse's hoof different from a cat's paw?

4. Variations:

   a. Describe it: Instead of using a photo, complete the same activity using an item. Your questions will prompt the children to describe the object's function, category, or whatever is appropriate.

   b. Nonfiction: Pictures from nonfiction books are especially effective. They provide an opportunity to reinforce science and social studies concepts and vocabulary while building oral language. This activity has the added benefit of helping students learn to use the photographs in nonfiction texts as a source of information (Stead, 2006).

Build a Cowboy

During our rodeo unit, my class often built a cowboy as part of the oral language component. I created simple cutouts of a cowboy hat, bandana, chaps, spurs, and boots. We began on Monday with our cowboy, dressed in jeans and a flannel shirt. I explained to the children that the cowboy's clothing served a purpose. I asked them to think about what cowboys do and why they would wear jeans instead of shorts or sweatpants, comparing jeans to the clothing the children were wearing. Through questioning, the children considered the durability of denim, as well as the protection it offered. Each day, we would add another piece to the cowboy's ensemble, discussing the use and function of each item. By the end of the week, the children were able to label a diagram of a cowboy correctly and write about the uses of various clothing items.

Just about anything in your curriculum that can be displayed as a diagram can be adapted for a Build It activity. For example:

1. **Build a Butterfly:** When doing a science unit on butterflies, you might build a butterfly by having cutouts of the various body parts, such as the wings, proboscis, antennae, and legs.

2. **Build a Healthy Meal:** After you have taught your students about the food pyramid and the basic food groups, you can use cutouts to plan a healthy, well-balanced meal.

3. **Centers:** Once the activity has been completed with the class, it can be placed in a center. Children also enjoy creating their own diagrams and explaining them to the class.

Mystery Bags

This activity develops critical thinking skills as well as expressive language. Students use questions and answers to correctly identify the mystery item. To introduce the activity, select a small item and place it in a brown lunch bag. Provide three to four clues about the item. You can structure the clues to include only adjectives, or you may include a category or other appropriate clues. Students ask questions about the item that can be answered with yes or no. They learn that they must listen to the questions asked by their classmates and remember the answers given, in order to figure out the mystery item.

Conclusion

Oral language development is an important component in a successful literacy program, but is crucial for the at-risk students you may have in your classroom. McGee and Richgels (2003) suggest that tape-recording your classroom discussions will help you determine the quality and quantity of your interactions and conversations with students. Are there places you could have asked questions to extend the conversation? Do you ask closed questions that your students answer with single-word responses? Is there evidence of rich and varied language and vocabulary?

When I took a hard look at my own patterns of interaction, I realized that I was missing many teachable moments. During the typical day, there were countless opportunities to infuse vocabulary and language development in ways that were meaningful, fun, and easy to implement.

The next chapter presents ways to take those everyday routines and occurrences and maximize the potential for teaching and learning vocabulary.

CHAPTER 3

Making Every Moment Count

Infusing Daily Routines With Rich Vocabulary

Learning vocabulary through the context of daily routines resembles the natural vocabulary acquisition process that children use to learn language at home. As students hear unfamiliar words used in familiar routines, they begin to develop concepts of the word meanings that they refine and revise through multiple exposures.

Daily routines present teachers with endless opportunities to infuse rich and varied vocabulary into the classroom experience (Dickinson & Tabors, 2001). A brief look at the way vocabulary can be infused into some typical classroom routines will open the door to a new way of thinking about the instructional potential of these typically mundane moments of the day.

Salutations: Greeting Your Students With Style

Take a tip from Charlotte, the original word-web wizard from E. B. White's *Charlotte's Web*. Greet your students with *salutations* instead of *good morning*!

Many teachers start the day by greeting their students at the door, shaking their hands, and welcoming them into the classroom. Instead of using the same language day after day, try a vocabulary infusion to add a little word power to the day. Like Charlotte, we can find unusual and fun ways to greet our students.

You will find that the children quickly begin to look forward to new ways of being greeted, and will begin to use the words as they greet you in the morning as well. Make a brief comment on the weather, a new outfit, an expression—and do it with unusual or interesting words:

- "Isn't this a glorious day?"
- "It looks rather gloomy out there this morning."
- "You look glum today—is everything all right?"

One of my responsibilities at school was morning car rider duty. Each day, one teacher was positioned in front of the school to help children out of their cars in an effort to keep the line moving quickly and ensure that the children were entering school safely. To make the job more pleasant for myself, I began greeting each child with a cheery good morning and making some little comment. "Hurry in quickly or you will be drenched!" "Good morning! You look bright and cheery today!" At first the children paid little attention to me. Many didn't respond or even make eye contact. But eventually, my persistent approach paid off. Children began to respond, often using the same expressions I'd used on another day. "You are going to get drenched today, Mrs. Kindle." Infusion at work.

The Daily Word: A New Use for the Morning Message

In many classrooms, the morning message is used as a means of modeling and reinforcing concepts about print for emergent and beginning readers. It can also be a way to infuse vocabulary. Previously introduced words can be used in a new context to expand word meaning. New words can be used with sufficient context clues that their meanings become clear. Because the word is presented in an authentic and meaningful context, it is a far more effective technique than the traditional word of the day, where students copy definitions (Hoyt, 2005).

Choose the daily word carefully, with opportunities for further use in mind. Introducing the word in the morning message can prepare the learners for a lesson later in the day. The theme or topic of your instruction will guide you in developing an extensive list of thematically based words from which to choose. Using words pulled from math, science, and social studies supports the development of content-area concepts.

After daily words are introduced and discussed in the morning message, they can be added to charts that are displayed in the writing center, to personal dictionaries, or on the word wall. It is important that the words be available to students for future reference.

Encourage students to use the daily word in their own journal writing, to listen for the teacher to use the word throughout the day, and to use it themselves in conversation. You can make a game of it by dividing your class into teams and keeping track with tally marks. Each time a student uses the word correctly in his writing or catches you saying the word, that team earns a point.

On subsequent days, consider using a derivative or alternate definition to deepen the children's understanding of the word's meaning and use.

March 16

Dear Boys and Girls,

Today we are going to <u>release</u> our butterflies. We will let them go in the park behind the school. Where do you think your butterfly will go when it is <u>released</u>?

Today is also an Early <u>Release</u> day, so school will be over at 10:45 this morning. Where will you go after school today?

Sincerely,
Mrs. Kindle

In this example, the daily word is *release*. On the previous day, the children were introduced to the word in the context of letting their butterflies go. Within this short message, the word release is used in another context as well. Because the message has been crafted to contain sufficient context clues, students are able to understand the subtle difference in the meanings. The concept of *release* could be further developed by brainstorming other things that might be released. For example, a student who goes fishing might be familiar with the concept of catch and release.

The message also presents opportunities for oral language development. Students can be asked to respond orally to the two questions: "Where do you think your butterfly will go when it is released?" and "Where will you go after school today?" Learning to answer in complete sentences is a skill that will help your students with written expression. Both questions could be developed in journal-writing activities later in the morning or in the week. As students use the daily words in their conversations and compositions, they develop a sense of ownership through authentic, contextualized use.

Move Expeditiously: Getting From Point A to Point B

Time spent lining up and walking from one place to another seems an unlikely time for vocabulary instruction. Yet even this most mundane of daily routines has instructional potential when it is infused with vocabulary. Look for new and interesting ways to tell your students to walk quickly and quietly.

My students particularly loved the word *expeditious*. One morning, the weather was threatening as I led my students out into the temporary building that housed our class. Before we left the main building, the rain started to fall. I told them we needed to move expeditiously, so that everyone would get in before it got too wet. Through the context, they understood that they needed to move quickly. When we got into the safety of our classroom, the students began asking if they had moved expeditiously enough—it was just a fun word for them to say. Later that morning, I had given the students a task to complete and told them they needed to work quickly, since our time was almost up. One boy raised his hand and said, "Don't you mean that we need to work expeditiously?"

A search for synonyms and antonyms will yield a wide variety of ways to express your usual directions in new and unusual ways.

walk	quickly	quietly
march	hastily	silently
file	rapidly	inaudibly
stride	swiftly	noiselessly

Of course, we aren't always moving quickly. On the playground, we may tell a student to *stroll* over to the bench and sit down, or *wander* around to find someone to play with.

The Cafeteria: A Smorgasbord of Adjectives

Having lunch duty with primary students is not for the faint of heart. Opening juice boxes and thermoses, dealing with the daily spills, and the logistics of getting large groups of children fed in 30 minutes is no picnic. It hardly seems to be a teachable moment. And yet, I found that using lunch as a time to infuse vocabulary was successful for the students, and made lunch duty enjoyable for me as well.

If you ask the average first grader how his lunch tastes, he will probably answer with the standard descriptor *good*. Lunches provide opportunities to build vocabulary that describes color, texture, aroma, and flavor. As you walk past your children, try commenting on their lunches to model the use of descriptive words.

- "The macaroni and cheese looks very creamy today."
- "The chicken smells scrumptious!"
- "Your chips have been pulverized! Did you crush your lunch bag?"
- "The carrots and celery sound fresh and crispy."

It won't take long before the children start asking you to comment on their lunches. They quickly begin to answer your questions about how their lunch tastes with adjectives other than good or bad.

Look for opportunities to review and apply learning from content areas. You can talk about food groups, nutrition, solids and liquids, and math.

- "What a healthy lunch! You have something from all of the food groups."
- "Did your mom cut your sandwich into halves or fourths?"
- "You need to eat your ice cream before it turns into a liquid!"

Calendar Time

If your daily instructional routine includes a calendar time, you can find many opportunities to infuse vocabulary. New and interesting words, presented within the context of a familiar routine, can energize the process and keep it from becoming dull and rote. When counting the number of days they have been in school, Jennifer tells her class that they could just count by ones, but that wouldn't be as *efficient* as counting by twos, fives, or tens. Using the word *efficient* is now part of the daily routine.

Marvelous Monday

Part of the typical calendar routine includes talking about the days of the week. Young children need practice with the concepts of yesterday, today, and tomorrow. Infuse vocabulary into the routine by adding alliterative adjectives.

Monday can be *marvelous, magnificent, magical, merry,* or *mysterious.* Tuesday can be *terrific, tantalizing, tenacious, terrible,* or *titanic.* Wednesday can be *wild, wacky, wonderful, whirlwind, winning, wintry, windy,* or *world-class.* Thursday can be *theatrical, thirsty, thinking, thoughtful, thrilling,* or *thunderous.* Friday can be *fantastic, fabulous, freaky, fanciful, fair, familiar, fantabulous, fascinating, fatiguing, favorable, festive, fine, first-rate, five-star, flexible, frisky, frolicking, frosty,* or just plain *fun!*

The Meteorologist's Report: Today's Weather

The weather portion of the calendar routine is an easy place to start infusing vocabulary. Brainstorm different ways that you can describe the temperature, the humidity, the rain, the heat, or the cold. Help your students learn the difference between a *gentle breeze* and *gusty winds.* As they describe the rain, ask them to talk about *mist, drizzle,* or a *downpour.* In my Houston home, we need to find new ways of saying hot and humid—our usual weather pattern.

Developing language of this type not only extends the breadth of a student's vocabulary but its depth as well. Understanding the gradation of meaning between *drizzle* and *deluge* will help students in the future with text comprehension and with their own writing as they seek just the right word to convey their thoughts (Hoyt, 2005).

Patterns: Crimson, Crimson, Cobalt

If your calendar routine includes a pattern of the day, infusing new vocabulary can be as easy as opening the crayon box. In a large box, you will find a handy resource for new names for familiar colors, and a wide variety of shades. Paint chips, available at local hardware and home improvement stores, are another great source for interesting shades and colors.

As a variation to color, try creating texture patterns (smooth, rough, sandy) or visual patterns (stripe, stripe, polka dots). You will find that your students can be imaginative and creative when it comes to this activity, which is exactly what you are hoping for!

Journal Writing

Daily journal writing is an important routine in any early literacy classroom (Morrow, 1997). Writing about things that are personally relevant gives students an authentic purpose in which to incorporate new and interesting vocabulary words. Make it easy for your students by posting word collections around the room. Some teachers prefer to create personal dictionaries for students to keep at their desks. Easily accessible references encourage the reluctant writer to take risks and try new words.

Add a structured sharing time to your routine. When a student shares his writing and uses an interesting word, point that out to the class.

> "I like the way you used the word *slither* when telling about how the snake moved. That really helped me make a picture in my mind of your story!"

If your students are like mine, for a while, everything will slither. But your continued comments on word choice will encourage other students to spice up their writing and to make attempts to use new vocabulary.

While one student is sharing his journal, promote active listening by asking the class to listen for specific types of words. You may ask for vivid verbs one day and colorful adjectives the next. Purposeful listening will improve your students' attention skills and heighten their awareness of language.

Morning Board Work

At many schools, it is common practice to have some type of work on the board for students to complete in the morning. This independent work is completed while the teacher handles the myriad tasks associated with starting the day. At my school, this typically consisted of a daily edit and a few math problems.

I just hate busywork! While I recognized the need to have my students engaged in something while I read notes from parents, filled out the lunch count, and collected book orders, I didn't want this time to be wasted. With a change in emphasis and a vocabulary infusion, our morning work became a stimulating and enjoyable part of the day. Here are a few examples that fit nicely into a morning work routine. All of these activities develop breadth of vocabulary, problem-solving abilities, and flexible thinking. The possibilities are limited only by your imagination.

Categories

Categories require students to look at a group of objects and find both similarities and differences. Students are actively engaged in determining the relationships between lexical items and in finding connections between new words and their prior knowledge. This ability is an essential component of vocabulary acquisition (Blachowicz & Fisher, 2000). Carefully planned categorization activities promote problem solving and flexible thinking.

Category activities can be done in a variety of ways. To keep things simple for morning work, I used a consistent format in which I would list four words on the board. Three of the words would be related in some way, while the fourth would not belong. When first introducing the activity, I made the connections obvious.

cat, dog, book, fish

Students had no difficulty determining that the book wasn't alive, and so it didn't belong. Children should be able to explain their answers. "The book doesn't belong because it isn't alive." Then they are ready for a more difficult task.

cat, dog, fish, hamster

Students: "But Mrs. Kindle, they are all alive!"

Mrs. Kindle: "You're right. So think about how they are the same and how one is different."

With a few prompts, the children are able to see that the fish lives in water, and so is in a different category than the cat, the dog, and the hamster.

Category activities frequently yield more than one possible answer. For example:

guitar, violin, flute, piano

One student responded that flute did not belong because all of the other instruments had strings. Another student argued that guitar didn't belong because it isn't part of the orchestra. Both students were right—and their different points of view benefited the entire class. (Note: This example took place in a second-grade classroom). Encourage your students to try to find more than one way to see the problem. Their creativity will amaze you!

The following examples show some of the variations that can be made to this activity. Changing the format frequently keeps the activity from becoming stale. Each variation requires a slightly different thought process. Always ask students to explain the reasons for their answers. Talking about their thinking is an important part of developing expressive vocabulary (Durso & Coggins, 1991). If your children are not yet reading, these activities can be done orally and pictures of the items can be placed in a pocket chart for students to see.

In Odd Man Out, students find the word that doesn't belong from a group of four listed on the board. For example:

plum, peach, orange, banana

This particular example sparked quite a debate. One student insisted that banana didn't belong because it had a different shape. Another student argued that the peach didn't belong because it was fuzzy. A third "out of the box" thinker suggested that the banana didn't belong because it doesn't have seeds. That discussion led to further reading to find out if "those little black things" were really seeds or not.

In What's My Rule?, students are given a list of three or four words and are asked to write a word or phrase that would most accurately name that category. For example:

cat, dog, fish, bird

While many students will respond with the obvious answer of *animals*, with careful questioning you can lead students to more specific categories, such as *pets*. Start with easy examples like the one given above and gradually increase the difficulty. You will be amazed at the connections your students can find!

Analogies

When your students have developed some skill with categories, analogies are a logical next step. Analogies can be used in oral language development, or as part of morning board work once the children become familiar with the task and have developed strategies for finding the relationships. By working with analogies, you can develop your students' depth and breadth of vocabulary knowledge (Greenwood, 2002). Additionally, working with analogies supports the development of reading comprehension and vocabulary, as students understand the connections and relationships between words and ideas (HuffBenkoski & Greenwood, 1995). Analogies require students to identify the relationship that exists between the first two terms in the set, and then extend that relationship to the second terms. Any of the terms that you have been developing in your day can be used.

Start with easy analogies:

Dog is to bark as duck is to _____.

Have your students extend the analogy to other animals and their sounds. If your students have difficulty, you can scaffold their learning by providing multiple choices for students to select from (Greenwood, 2002). Do not settle for the "right" answer. Require your students to explain their responses. Have them identify the relationship between the terms. While it may seem an unnecessary step, verbalizing the thinking process will support the learners as they encounter more difficult tasks and support the less capable students by reinforcing the process, not just the product.

HuffBenkoski and Greenwood (1995) suggest developing stem, or bridge, sentences that describe the relationships between two words. In our sample analogy, we would lead the children to construct a statement, either orally or in writing.

A dog barks. A duck quacks.

This practice helps students begin to think about the relationship between sentences and ideas. These relationships are important in recognizing organizational structures of text and they also facilitate comprehension.

Brainstorming, Synonyms, and Antonyms

Other possible morning activities include brainstorming and generating synonyms and antonyms. Have children brainstorm lists of words that fit in certain categories or themes. For example, you might have them think of as many words as they can that would fit the category of *school supplies* at the beginning of the year, or words related to *weather*, when studying weather in science. Animal names, foods, actions, and colors are just a few categories you may want to use. As your children become more skilled, try some more complex categories, such as "things that are round," or "things that water is used for." The lists can be generated individually, in pairs, in groups, or as a whole class.

Synonyms and antonyms help children understand word meanings. It is easy to incorporate practice with synonyms and antonyms into your morning work activities. Simple matching exercises are a good place to start, but your students will soon be able to generate their own synonyms and antonyms. Encourage them to use classroom lists or unusual words they have encountered in their reading or heard outside of the classroom. Another activity is to provide four words, three of which are synonyms, and ask the children to find the word that does not belong. For example you might write *large, immense, tiny, giant* on the board. Your children may not know the meaning of *immense*, but since they will likely know that *tiny* and *large* are antonyms, they learn through the exercise that *immense* must be similar to *large* and *giant*.

Triple Plays

One of the difficulties in working with synonyms is that they often have shades of meaning that are important for children to understand. If a child uses a thesaurus to find a more interesting word for *bite* to use in his writing, he may find *chew, chomp,* and *gnaw.* Despite their underlying similarity, these words are different enough in meaning that they cannot be used interchangeably in every context. The activity that follows is helpful in drawing students' attention to these very important nuances of meaning.

This activity can be done as a whole group with the teacher as scribe, in groups, or individually. For younger students who have difficulty writing, or for students who lack a breadth of vocabulary to handle the task independently, the whole-group format works best. As your students develop their skills and broaden their vocabularies, the shift can be made to small groups or individual completion.

To introduce Triple Plays, ask your students to generate a few synonyms for the word *big.* Most classes will quickly generate a list that includes common words like *large, giant, huge, gigantic,* and *enormous.* Create a three-column chart on the board. Put a minus sign at the top of the left column and a plus sign at the top of the right column.

Using a script similar to the one that follows, guide your students through the process.

> *"Boys and girls, if you were really hungry, you might ask your mom for a huge piece of cake."* (Write the word *huge* in the center column.)
>
> *"If you were really, really hungry, you might ask mom for an enormous piece of cake."* (Write the word *enormous* in the right column.)
>
> *"If you were just a little bit hungry, you may only want a big piece."* (Write the word *big* in the left column.)
>
> *"Even though these three words are all very similar, they don't mean exactly the same thing. Big is smaller than huge, and enormous would be even bigger than huge."*

Once your students have the idea, they are ready to try Triple Plays individually or in pairs. Have the students fold a sheet of paper into three columns and place the plus and minus signs at the top of the right and left columns. Give them several words to write in the center column. It is a good idea to provide a word bank for your students' first attempts at Triple Plays. As they gain familiarity with the task, you can allow them to generate their own responses. Some students enjoy creating their own Triple Plays to pose to the class. They are excited and proud to see their problems on the board the next day for other students to solve.

Here are some examples:

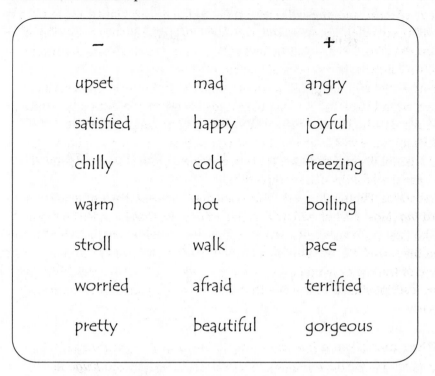

−		+
upset	mad	angry
satisfied	happy	joyful
chilly	cold	freezing
warm	hot	boiling
stroll	walk	pace
worried	afraid	terrified
pretty	beautiful	gorgeous

This activity can be done as a group during a morning meeting at first, and then can be used as board work or in a center as the children develop their skills. More uses of the versatile activity can be found in Chapter 6.

1. Create three columns on a chart or the board.
2. Mark the left column with a minus (–) sign and the right column with a plus (+) sign.
3. Write a familiar word in the center.
4. Have students generate synonyms or similar words that vary in degree from each term that you provide.

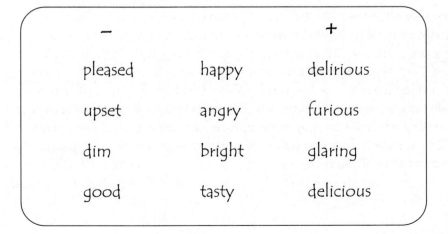

−		+
pleased	happy	delirious
upset	angry	furious
dim	bright	glaring
good	tasty	delicious

Triple Plays can also be used to help students understand the positive and negative connotations associated with some words. When children begin to use the thesaurus to find synonyms to use in their writing, they often select words without considering how a word's connotations can change the meaning of a phrase or sentence. This activity can help heighten students' awareness of how word choice can affect meaning.

In this variation, the left column with the minus sign becomes the negative side and the right column is the positive side. The word placed in the center should be as neutral as possible.

Using a children's thesaurus, such as Level 1 of *The Writer's Thesaurus* (Pasquarella, 2003), have your students look up a common word such as *difficult*. They will find entries such as *hard, puzzling, challenging, complicated,* and *troublesome*. The word *difficult* is fairly neutral, so it belongs in the center column. Through your questioning, guide students to understand the different connotations of words such as *challenging* and *troublesome*. For example, you might point out that the root word *trouble* in *troublesome* has a negative connotation:

- "Would you rather solve a difficult problem in math, or a troublesome one?"

- "Here is a challenging math problem for you to solve. Doesn't that make the problem sound more interesting than just plain hard?"

I would much rather be described as *mature* than *old*, and I certainly am not ready to be considered *elderly*! While this variation of Triple Plays is designed for use with older students, even your very young ones can benefit from an occasional lesson. A list of suggested Triple Plays is included in Appendix C at the end of this book.

Recess

Recess seems an unlikely time to think about vocabulary development, but even outdoor play and free time can provide opportunities for vocabulary infusion.

One of my favorite things about recess is having the time to talk with students informally about the things that are important to them. This is a time when you can develop language skills by asking thoughtful questions and modeling attentive listening (Mountain, 2000). McGee and Richgels (2003) consider these informal, one-on-one conversations to be a crucial component in language development. And of course, you can look for opportunities to infuse the conversation with a little vocabulary.

For instance, teachers of young children know their students are always finding "treasures" on the playground. Use the opportunity to ask them questions about the texture of that special rock, the fragrance of the wildflower. But be prepared! The attention you give to a unique and colorful pebble will likely result in 22 children scouring the playground for rocks. So be ready for lots of teachable moments!

Infusing Vocabulary Into Outdoor Games

These activities take advantage of young learners' natural inclination to get moving! Games that develop large motor skills (and burn off some of that energy) can be played to reinforce vocabulary learned in the classroom. Many concepts that are difficult to describe in words are easy to understand when there is a movement connected to them.

Mother, May I?

The familiar children's game Mother, May I? can be adapted to a game that reinforces vocabulary. Students demonstrate their growing word knowledge as they respond to "Mother's" directions.

1. One student is selected to be Mother.
2. The remaining students line up facing Mother at a predetermined distance.
3. Mother calls a name and tells that child to move forward a given number of steps, using key vocabulary words. For example: "Susan, you may leap forward three times."
4. Before the student can move forward, he must first ask, "Mother, may I?"
5. The student may then move forward, *leaping, hopping, twirling,* in the manner chosen by Mother.
6. The first student to reach Mother wins and takes her place.

Relay Races

Relay races can be infused with vocabulary. Write appropriate verbs on cards and place them in a basket. Select a student to be the starter. The starter selects a card from the basket, announces the word, and demonstrates the action to the class. The starter (along with the teacher) watches to be sure that all students perform the selected action correctly as they run the relay.

Obstacle Course

Help students understand position words by developing an obstacle course. For example, instruct students to go *down* the slide, *up* the ladder, *around* the swings, *through* the tunnel, and so on. Select a student to be a play-by-play announcer to involve everyone in the process.

Conclusion

Can you see the possibilities of vocabulary infusion for your daily routines? Are you ready to get started? Select one part of your day as a starting point. As your comfort level increases, you will begin to see the possibilities to enrich vocabulary throughout your day.

Jennifer completes her lunch count each day by having her children raise their hands to indicate their choice: "Raise your hand if you want chicken nuggets." When the entire class made the same choice one day, she announced, "It's unanimous." Through her creative infusion of vocabulary, her students have a new word and a new routine.

I recently visited Jennifer's class during lunch count. She asked the children to stand if they were buying lunch. Opening the lunch count folder, she said, "Today for lunch we have the fabulous favorite . . ." (The anticipation was evident in the faces of the children.) "Breakfast for lunch!" She asked each child to indicate if he or she wanted breakfast for lunch, or the second choice of a chef's salad. As she went around the room, you could sense the excitement building. Would there be a unanimous choice today? Finally the spell was broken as a child ordered a chef's salad. The vote would not be unanimous that day. Jennifer has succeeded in turning a dull, boring routine into an exciting and language-filled moment.

It's easy, it's fun, and it works!

CHAPTER 4

Using Centers to Assess and Promote Language Development

Center activities are an important part of a quality early childhood program. For our youngest learners, this time provides opportunities to explore, imagine, and create. The informal peer interactions that occur as children work and play in centers provide a backdrop for language use that encourages participation from the most reluctant speakers.

For children in the primary grades, centers typically take the form of work stations with specific instructional tasks built into the design. Students work together to solve problems and complete tasks that can be structured to meet their specific academic levels and needs. And where children are working together, there will be language! Take advantage of the opportunity to maximize the word learning and language potential of center activities.

Centers provide young children with much-needed space to talk. Students have the opportunity to interact with peers and to develop listening and speaking skills in an informal, natural manner. Center time also provides the opportunity for you to have one-on-one or informal conversations with your children. Using the strategies of questioning, extending, recasting, and repetition, these informal interactions can be an important way to develop your students' expressive language skills (McGee & Richgels, 2003).

A Risk-Free Place to Play With Language

Children who are very shy or are just acquiring the language may be intimidated by speaking to the whole class or to you as the teacher. For these children, centers provide a risk-free environment to test out their developing language skills.

In the ESL literature, this is known as the *willingness to communicate* (MacIntyre, Baker, Clement & Donovan, 2003). Sometimes, a child is capable of communicating, but chooses not to. He may be afraid of saying the wrong thing and being punished or ridiculed. He may be extremely shy. He may have cultural constraints on speaking aloud in class. There are many factors that play into just how willing a child is to talk in the classroom setting.

Antonio was a kindergarten student who attended my ESL summer school class one summer. During class routines, such as the morning calendar, Antonio would not participate, regardless of how much scaffolding I supplied and how carefully I structured the experience for him to ensure success. He would simply stare at me with big brown eyes and say nothing. I was very concerned about his progress and assumed, as many teachers would, that he did not understand enough English to know what was going on in the lesson.

When I incorporated an abbreviated center time into our daily routine, Antonio seemed just as reluctant to participate. I made a habit of visiting the centers as the children were working and engaging them in conversation about their play. Antonio would never answer my questions or respond to my comments.

One day, as I talked to the children playing in a nearby center, I overheard a child giving directions on the way the building blocks should be arranged. "No, it needs to go up here to make the roof." Without moving closer, I turned my head, and was amazed to see that Antonio was directing the play of the children in the block center.

I discovered that my presence inhibited Antonio's expressive language. His willingness to communicate was limited to peer interactions where he felt comfortable. I began carefully interacting with him in this context. I would comment on what he was doing, but not ask questions that demanded an answer. Gradually, he began to talk to me not only during centers, but also in the more formal instructional setting as well.

If I had not observed this behavior, I would have continued to hold an inaccurate impression of Antonio's oral language capabilities. I realized that I would need an additional means of evaluating my students.

Assessing Language Development During Center Time

Center time presents a unique opportunity for you to observe and assess your students' use of language in an authentic setting. Two measurements used to evaluate the complexity of children's oral language are number of different words (NDW) and mean length of utterance (MLU) (Owens, 2001). In these measures, samples of children's speech are taken and analyzed, providing a holistic measure of their language ability.

NDW consists of the number of different words used in a given speech sample. Higher NDWs indicate a larger expressive vocabulary.

The MLU is determined by counting the number of morphemes present in each of the child's sentences. Dividing the total number of morphemes in the sample by the number of sentences gives you the MLU for the sample. Because the MLU is an average, it provides a more accurate picture of the child's use of language than a single sentence.

Morphemes are the smallest units of meaning in language. These units may be words, such as *tree* or *car*, or word parts, such as *s, ing,* or *ed*, and are classified as free or bound. A word that can stand alone, like *cat*, is a free morpheme. The second type of morpheme is the bound morpheme. A bound morpheme is a word part that conveys meaning, such as the *-s* to indicate a plural, or *un-* to indicate the negative. Bound morphemes cannot stand alone and must be attached to a free morpheme. For example, by adding the bound morphemes to the word *cat*, a two-morpheme word *cats* is formed.

Let's look at the example of Antonio's sentence mentioned above. "No, it needs to go up here to make the roof." This sentence contains 11 free morphemes—*no, it, need, to, go, up, here, to, make, the, roof*—and one bound morpheme, the *-s* on *needs*. With 12 morphemes, this is a fairly complex sentence! If Antonio had merely said, "No, here," that would have only been two morphemes.

Assessing MLU and NDW at various checkpoints throughout the year will allow you to monitor the progress that your students are making in developing their oral language and increasing their vocabularies. A simple form, such as the one on the page 46, can be used to track students' progress.

Instructional decisions can be made after determining areas of strength and weakness. While it would be ideal to acquire samples for all of your students, it is not likely to be practical for you to do so. Focus on the children with the greatest need. If you are fortunate enough to have an instructional aide, you may be able to use his or her assistance in gathering the language samples for these children.

Name	Date	Sample	Number of Sentences	MLU	NDW
Antonio	11/15/07	No, it needs to go up here to make the roof.	2	7 ½	13
Susan	11/16/07	Give me. No. Here.	3	1	4

Collecting the Samples

Language samples can easily be collected during center time. Set up a tape recorder to capture the conversations as children work in their centers, or you can observe the children at play and script their comments. Both methods have advantages and disadvantages.

Using a Tape Recorder

Tape-recording allows you to acquire extended samples and frees you up to conduct other tasks. Since you do not have to be physically present with this method, it allows you to capture authentic peer exchanges. For extremely reticent speakers like Antonio, this may be the best way to get an accurate picture of language use. The children quickly forget about the tape recorder as they get engrossed in their play.

Tape-recording is not without challenges. It is sometimes quite difficult to determine the identity of the speaker from a group of two or three children. And children do not always wait for others to stop talking before they chime in. Additionally, without observing the context and the nature of the interaction, it can be difficult to understand exactly what the child is saying, making the accurate transcription of the tape and subsequent analysis challenging.

Scripting Observed Language

Anecdotal scripts require your immediate presence and take your full attention. This can be difficult in a classroom of active children. The greatest advantages of this method are that you can easily follow the conversation and you have the opportunity to join in. This allows you to pose questions to clarify the child's comments, or to extend the conversation to acquire a lengthier sample.

After you have scripted or transcribed several sentences, you simply calculate the number of morphemes in each utterance and the number of different words used. By charting the MLU and NDW for your students, you will have a means of tracking their language development through the school year. This information can guide you as you plan for effective instruction.

You may even hear some infusion words popping up spontaneously in your students' play!

Using Assessment Data to Plan Instruction

The information that you obtain from the informal assessment of oral language can serve as a guide for your instruction. The process involves analyzing the child's strengths and weaknesses and then identifying one or two key objectives to target for instruction. The instructional plan may be quite simple and consist of a few target behaviors that you structure into your interactions with the child. Let's consider how this might look for Antonio and Susan, the students in the sample described above.

The language sample collected for Antonio shows that he was using a lot of different words and his sentences contained many morphemes. His language and vocabulary seemed to be developing well, yet he did not participate in class or talk to the teacher. The instructional plan for Antonio might include frequent visits by the teacher to his center to engage him in nonthreatening conversations about what he is doing.

Susan's sample shows limited language use. In three sentences she used only four morphemes and four different words. Susan loves getting attention from the teacher, so a plan for Susan might include spending a few minutes with her each day during lunchtime or recess, using questioning strategies to draw more language out of her.

The instructional plans can be simple, yet still be effective in promoting language development. The time and effort involved in gathering and analyzing the samples will pay off when you see the growth that occurs.

Infusing Vocabulary Into Existing Centers

Chances are you already have some type of centers established in your classroom. Centers that are routinely used in kindergarten classrooms include the kitchen or home living area, blocks, art, puzzles, dramatic play, and literacy activities. In primary classrooms, centers typically shift in structure and content and may take the form of work stations featuring literacy activities. Frequently, math and science centers take the place of blocks, kitchen, art, and puzzles. Even if you do not have a formal center time, you may have a series of activities arranged for students to work on while you meet with small groups for guided reading.

What makes infusion centers different? With a little thought and effort on your part, centers can be structured in ways that encourage language use and development. Design tasks that require students to explain their thinking, express their feelings, or describe their product. Add props and materials that foster the use of newly learned vocabulary words.

In most cases, the center activities suggested in this chapter will use materials you already have available in your classroom. Many activities that have been introduced in large-group activities can also be used effectively in centers. For example, the crayon box activities described in the previous chapter can be structured for a small group. Further word learning is supported by the additional exposures and practice. The rest of this chapter offers ideas for turning traditional centers into infusion centers.

Masterpiece Theater

The theater center can be used for reenactments of familiar stories or the creation of original scripts. As children act out favorite fairy tales or stories read in class, they are engaged in the important literacy skills of summarization, sequencing, and characterization. In fact, many of the commonly used primary benchmarks use retelling as the vehicle for assessing reading comprehension in beginning readers. When children are engaged in creating their own scripts, they have many opportunities to develop vocabulary and oral language skills.

By making a tape recorder available, this center activity has the added bonus of providing a recording that can later be analyzed for MLU and NDW, or as a baseline sample for future comparison. The drama center can be as simple or elaborate as you choose to make it. The three ideas shared below are some examples to get you started.

1. **Puppet Theater:** Place a variety of puppets in the center, or you can have the students make their own. I have used finger puppets that I purchased for a few dollars at a local discount store. The puppets might specifically go with a story that has been read. For example, when reading books in the Frog and Toad series, I had my second graders make Frog and Toad puppets. They used the puppets to create new story lines or to retell their favorite episodes. Children can record their stories or perform them for the class.

2. **Lights, Camera, Action:** Provide students in the center with a variety of scenarios to act out. For prereaders, set the stage for action as you introduce the center for the week. Brainstorm possible scripts that they can develop. For example, they may take the roles of

customer, waiter, and chef in a restaurant. Provide simple props for younger children, or give a list of vocabulary words for the older children to incorporate into their skit. Your list might include words such as *menu, appetizer, beverage,* and *dessert*. The goal is to incorporate all of the target words (or props) into their skit.

3. **Today's News:** Students can prepare a news report to share with the class. They can tell about the important news of the day, the cafeteria menu, and the weather.

Make It and Take It in the Art Center

Art projects that require your students to follow a specific series of directions provide opportunities to develop specialized vocabulary. Time-order words, such as *first, next, then,* and *last*, are an integral part of these activities as students follow the steps in sequence. Children can review math concepts as they fold their papers into fourths, or glue the circle on the square and the triangle beside the rectangle. By varying the types of activities, many of the concept vocabulary words of math and science can be reinforced and used in an authentic manner. As a bonus, many of these projects can also be turned into writing activities as students record how they made a particular craft.

Collect a variety of simple art projects. Ideas can be found in magazines for teachers, or you can ask your art teacher for suggestions. Write step-by-step directions for the project inside a manila folder. Use rebus sentences or appropriate illustrations to support less proficient readers. All of the materials needed to make the project are precut and stored in small plastic bag inside the folder. If you have parent volunteers at your school, this a great project to ask them to do for you. You can put out one folder per week, or place several in the center and allow students to choose their project.

Welcome to the Construction Corner

Most kindergarten classrooms have block centers, but they are seldom seen in first or second grade. Many classrooms do not have the space to accommodate blocks, and the value of this activity, which looks a lot like simple play time, may not be apparent for the older primary student. But with a little planning and creativity, a block center can be incorporated into your classroom.

The block center is a great place to develop vocabulary. When children select the right-shaped block for their construction, they revisit the math vocabulary of geometry as they handle rectangles, cylinders, squares, and triangular prisms. Position words, such as *over, beside, on,* or *next to*, appear in conversations as students explain their ideas to their classmates. Give your students the opportunity to present their designs to the class, describing their unique features.

Students become architects as they design offices, apartment buildings, and homes. They can become aerospace engineers and design the next space shuttle. Collect photographs of buildings that you can display for inspiration and label them with words like *mansion, castle, skyscraper, tower, apartment complex*. When appropriate, you can tailor the construction task to match topics you discuss in other parts of the day. For example, as you read books about space for science, you can ask your students to design a space station or a new planetary rover. A discussion about farm animals might lead to the building of barns and silos.

Large sets of wooden blocks are not always an option, but Legos or other small building sets will work as well. In fact, for some projects, snap-together blocks are preferable because they allow your students to create more intricate designs. You may have some at home that your children no longer play with, or you may be able to find someone willing to donate a set to your class.

Make a binder called "Project Designs." Students can record their designs as blueprints to be kept in the center for other students to recreate. Younger students can draw and label; older students can write step-by-step directions for building their design.

The Science Lab

In the science lab, children have an opportunity to investigate, explore, and discover. Although science content and vocabulary are the focus for infusion, math concepts are also incorporated as your students measure and record the length and weight of specimens. Describing objects encourages the use of precise adjectives to record texture and color.

Provide your students with a selection of interesting objects to explore. These objects might be related to your units of study in science, or just interesting things you have collected. Parents can be a great resource by loaning items of interest they have collected. The shark jaw that my son purchased as a souvenir on a trip to the beach was a favorite of my class during our ocean unit.

Outfit your lab with the tools of the trade. Magnifying glasses, balance scales for weighing items, and rulers for measuring length help your students conduct their investigations. Many of the science objectives for young children involve the processes rather than content. The science lab provides your students with opportunities to engage in the processes of science as they observe and explore. They practice the language of science as they record their observations in field notes. Children can record their field notes in written form in a science journal, or they can tape-record them. Tape-recording provides a means of assessing knowledge without having to rely on writing ability, and also provides you with a language sample to analyze for MLU and NDW, as described in the previous chapter. Here are a few suggested activities that foster oral language and vocabulary acquisition in the science center:

1. **What Is It?:** Place an item in the center that is not easily identifiable to your students. Using the materials in the center, your little scientists are charged with the task of discovering the identity of the item. Guide them in their explorations with key questions, or provide clues along the way.

2. **Describe It:** The task in this activity is to describe the item as completely as possible. Students work to accurately record the size of the object by recording its length and weight. They describe its texture, color, and composition. Provide a recording sheet with specific items to include in their description. Lists of texture words along with samples will help your students find just the right word to describe how the item feels. Color chips from the paint store can help them identify the exact shade of brown.

3. **Compare Them:** Place two objects in the lab for your students to compare and contrast. You may ask them to record their observations on a Venn diagram. Math concepts of greater, less than, longer, and shorter are used as children identify and describe differences between the objects. Comparative adjectives are used as they describe differences in color and texture.

Math Centers

Math centers can be infused easily with vocabulary. Activities can be structured in ways that provide exposure to novel words and content-specific vocabulary as students practice math concepts. Many children can master math computations, but struggle with the vocabulary they encounter in word problems. Incorporating opportunities for students to practice the language of math is key to their success.

Word Problems

Students can solve word problems that feature new vocabulary words, or you can provide them with a word bank to use in creating their own story problems. The word bank may be developed with help from the class during a unit of study, or after reading a particular text. For example, you may share *Ten Sly Piranhas: A Counting Story in Reverse (A Tale of Wickedness—and Worse!)* by William Wise.

> *Ten sly piranhas were swimming in the river,*
> *Ten hungry fishes, hoping very much to dine.*
> *Then one sly piranha sneaked up close behind another,*
> *And with a gulp, and a gurgle—*
> *There were only nine.*

Armed with a list of animals found in the rain forest, your students will enjoy writing their own word problems. Using their imagination and creativity deepens their understanding of how the language used in word problems signals the operations of addition, subtraction, multiplication, and division.

Nonfiction texts, such as *All About Owls* by Jim Arnosky (1995), provide additional sources for word problems. This text includes a page featuring illustrations and facts about several species of owls. Students can create word problems comparing owl lengths. For example:

- How much longer is the snowy owl than the long-eared owl?
- Which owl is the smallest? The largest?
- Place the owls in order from the smallest to the largest.

Patterns

The ability to identify, extend, and create patterns figures prominently in the primary math curriculum. Practice with patterns constructed of colors, shapes, and objects prepares children for the more abstract number patterns they will encounter. Infusing this kind of vocabulary is simple to accomplish. For example:

- Create and label an ABC pattern using animals found in the ocean.
- Create and label an AABA pattern using two shades of blue (from the crayon box or paint chips).
- Miss Rumphius wants to plant her favorite colors of lupines so that they create a pattern in her garden. If she has blue, rose, lavender, and peach lupine seeds, what are some of the patterns she can create? (Read *Miss Rumphius* by Barbara Cooney, 1985.)

Charts, Graphs, and Tables

Learning to read graphic forms of information is critical for success in mathematics. On standardized tests, our students must be able to answer questions based on facts presented in the form of line graphs, bar graphs, pictographs, tables and charts, and other formats.

1. **Creating Graphs:** This activity can go way beyond making graphs of the various ways students are going home after school. Graphs can be created to illustrate a wide variety of information related to your units of study as well as to develop vocabulary. Younger students might sort and graph sets of plastic animals from the rain forest, farm, or ocean. Older students might create a graph of the number of moons for each planet.

2. **Reading Tables:** After reading books on Antarctica or penguins, find or create a table that gives information about various types of penguins. Have your students rank the penguins in order of height or

weight, from least to greatest. Prepare a series of questions about penguins for them to answer using the information in the table as a guide. Many nonfiction books, such as the Magic School Bus series, provide tables or charts that can be used. For example, the *Magic School Bus Explores the World of Bugs* contains a chart comparing insects and spiders. Students can use this chart to answer teacher-developed questions, or they can write their own questions for other classmates to solve.

Literacy Centers

Literacy centers are a natural setting for vocabulary development. The resource materials provided with many basal reading programs include ideas that are adaptable to center use. Additionally, many commercially developed games and activities can broaden and deepen your students' word knowledge as they are exposed to new words and encounter new meanings for familiar words.

Many of the infusion activities described throughout this book can be placed in centers for small groups of children to enjoy. Once the procedures have been introduced and are understood by the class, center use provides students with increased opportunities for participation and practice. For example, the Hangman game described in the previous chapter can easily be played by a small group of children in a literacy center. Provide them with a list of previously learned words to choose from, or you can let them choose words they have encountered on their own.

In addition, with a few modifications, vocabulary can become an emphasized feature in your existing literacy centers. Most primary classrooms have a cozy library corner for children to relax and enjoy independent reading. By posting charts of word collections on the wall, or creating a binder for word lists, your students can have a place to record new words they discover. Children who enjoy looking at nonfiction books can record the names of new animals they find. Proficient readers may find words to add to your class lists of Vivid Verbs or Amazing Adjectives.

Sorting and Categorizing Words

Lists of words generated during brainstorming sessions can be cut apart for sorting and categorization activities. Develop flexibility of thinking in your students as you extend the work done in a classification exercise during your morning board work by using the same list of words and asking your students to categorize them in a different way. Or you might use an open sort technique, and have the students place the words in two or three groups and then determine and label their own categories.

Writing

Other activities described throughout the book adapt easily to the writing center as well. For example, after students have created a Make It and Take It project in the art center, they may write down the directions so they can make another project at home. Children enjoy reading and solving riddles, but they also enjoy writing them. As your young authors are penning their own riddles, jokes, and hink pinks, they develop their writing and spelling skills as well as practice using language in a playful and creative way.

Conclusion

The use of centers in the primary grades meets the social, emotional, and instructional needs of our young learners. Children need time to talk to develop their language skills. The small-group setting provides a risk-free environment for children to try out new words and language patterns. Opportunities for practice increase as the number of children in the group decrease. They learn how to verbalize their thinking as they work together to solve problems.

From the infusion perspective, centers provide you with a great opportunity to provide additional exposure to novel vocabulary in a context that promotes authentic and meaningful use.

CHAPTER 5

Weaving Vocabulary Into Literacy Activities

I thought I was doing a fairly good job teaching vocabulary. Early in my career, literature-based approaches and thematic units were commonly used. Like many of my colleagues, I purchased books containing ready-to-teach units and followed the recommendations of the authors for vocabulary words to teach. After all, they were the experts, weren't they?

As my district made the shift back to a basal series, I again relied on the authors to tell me which words to focus on for vocabulary instruction. The series included tips for teaching the words, workbook pages for practice, and assessments. It certainly made it easy, but I was left with a nagging feeling that something was missing.

It is no wonder that my students considered vocabulary to be something you do; a part of the daily routine, like the morning announcements. Frankly, it was boring and meaningless. How could I take the words I was required to teach, get them off the page, and into the lives of my students?

My best students could correctly identify the words, fill in the blanks, and match definitions. But the next week we would start on a new group of words and never see last week's words again. It hardly seemed worth their effort.

For other students, these activities did little to develop their word knowledge and they struggled make sense of a disjointed group of words they would never see again. At best, my students might recognize a word they encountered in reading: "That was on our vocabulary list."

Wouldn't it make sense for me to teach words that would be useful to the children in their reading and writing? I didn't know it at the time, but what I was looking for were the words that Beck, McKeown, and Kucan (2002) call Tier 2 words—the high-utility words of mature language users.

For most of us, the reading and writing parts of our day are the easiest place to start changing the way we approach vocabulary instruction. In this chapter, we will look some ways to maximize the word learning potential of literacy activities you already have in your daily instructional routine. By infusing exposure to novel words into reading, writing, and even phonological and phonemic awareness activities, vocabulary instruction can become part of the fabric of the day rather than an isolated component.

Reading to and With Your Students

The benefits of reading to children have long been recognized by teachers, parents, and researchers. Read-alouds and shared reading support your instruction by allowing you to model comprehension strategies and fluent reading, build background knowledge, develop concepts, and share your love of books. Students are exposed to the language of books, which may be substantially different from their daily oral language. Concepts about print are developed as children experience text in the highly supportive context of shared reading (Tompkins, 2006).

When students have had a lot of exposure to the language of books, it is evident in their writing as well. The following example was composed by Crissy, an economically disadvantaged first grader. As she writes an original version of "Jack and the Beanstalk," she demonstrates her understanding of the fairy tale genre and her familiarity with the traditional version of the classic tale.

Once upon a time there was a poor and lonely family. When Jack's mother said Jack old snow white has run out of milk for us to drick and butter for our bred so we got to sale her. So Jack set off to sale her. Wile Jack wondered he cam upon a srange person who said Jack what a butiful caw you got there would you like this wouderful magic blanket. Jack was fond at the magic blanket so he took it. When Jack got home he said I got a magic blanket. His mother got so mad she sent Jack to his room. When Jack woke up he saw the magic blanket flying all over the house. Jack was so amazed that he was up an about and got on the magic blanket and out the door he went. Whay outside up up up went the magic blanket all the whay up to the sky passed the clouds till Jack saw a butiful house. Jack was hungry he wondred if they sad some breckfest to eat so he got off the magic blanket and walked to the house and nocked on the door a very pretty women opened the door. Jack asked the women if he can have something to eat the woman said yes but watch out for my husband Jafar he likes to eat kids like you. So Jack went inside to eat when Jack head somebody way women! Give me something to eat! The women said hear hide in the closet the man said bring my magic goose who laid silver eggs and my gold! When Jafar said FE! FI! FO! FUM! I smell the blood of an Englishman shen Jafar feel asleep Jack stold the gold and went home so qickly that his falmily lived happily evey apter.

Crissy incorporated traditional phrases from fairy tales, such as *once upon a time* and *they lived happily ever after*. She stuck closely to the storyline of the well-known version, but substituted new elements, such as the magic carpet in lieu of magic beans, and the goose that laid silver eggs, not golden ones. The influence of other stories she had heard and seen is evident in the way she imported the magic carpet and the name Jafar from the popular *Aladdin* movie that had just come out.

The benefits of reading aloud are obvious, yet we often get so busy juggling all of the bits and pieces required for a balanced literacy program that devoting a block of time each day to reading aloud to our students seems a luxury we can't afford.

I often found myself using read-alouds to fill those awkward moments before and after lunch or at the close of the day. I put little thought into it, typically just grabbing a book off the shelf and away we went. Over time I realized I was wasting precious moments to tap into the power and potential of reading aloud. I got serious about the process, selecting texts with purpose, and planning the vocabulary I would target for instruction.

Children's books are also a treasure trove of vocabulary. Hayes and Ahrens (1988) found that the number of rare words found in the average piece of children's literature exceeds the number found in conversations between college graduates. If we hope to extend the vocabulary of our students, reading to them should be an essential part of our day.

Effective Practice for Reading Aloud to Students

Although the storybook reading context has long been recognized as a vital means of exposing children to novel vocabulary words, effective strategies for instruction have been less clear. We do know that children need repeated exposures to new words in a variety of meaningful contexts to develop their word knowledge.

Repeated readings

Biemiller and Boote (2006), in a study of kindergarten students, found that simply reading a particular text several times increased vocabulary knowledge—even without any direct instruction in word meaning. When repeated readings were paired with instruction, the gains were even greater.

As you read texts to your students, call their attention to unfamiliar words and supply a simple, concise definition.

Text: And not content, it took a hat, and still not satisfied with that, (Excerpt from *The Wind Blew* by Pat Hutchins)

Teacher: "Content means 'happy with'—the wind wasn't content, it still wanted more!"

If the word is represented in the illustration, you might simply point to the picture while saying the word.

Text: It plucked a hanky from a nose and up and up and up it rose. (Excerpt from *The Wind Blew* by Pat Hutchins)

Teacher: (*points to the hanky in the illustration*)

You will want to plan ahead so that you minimize the interruptions to the story. Five or six key words will be enough to target. Script your definitions on sticky notes and place them on the appropriate pages. After you have read the story a few times, you will no longer need the aids, and the process will become a natural part of your reading style.

Repetition in Multiple Contexts

In addition to repeated readings, look for opportunities to infuse the target vocabulary words throughout the day. These additional exposures deepen the child's knowledge of the word by presenting it in a new context and providing examples of authentic use. For example, if you read *The Wind Blew* on a windy day, take advantage of your recess time to point out to your children how the wind is *whipping* the leaves off the trees, or how it *swept* up the dirt under the swings to form a dust devil. These teachable moments lift the words off the pages of the book and swirl them into the lives of your students.

Vocabulary Games and Activities

In addition to the definitions you provide during reading and the spontaneous use of the words throughout the day, you will also want to plan some focused instruction for your students. Many activities can be planned to strengthen your students' knowledge in a hands-on manner that gets them actively engaged in constructing meaning. Research tells us that this approach is far more effective than copying definitions from the dictionary in promoting vocabulary development.

Line It Up

Line It Up, an activity that provides practice for target vocabulary words in a game-like format, is a class favorite. You may follow the format suggested here, but you will soon begin to make variations to reflect the particular words you have chosen for study, to meet the needs of your students. *The Wind Blew* by Pat Hutchins (1993) was used in the following example.

Day 1—Select five to seven words for study: *snatched, swept, content, whipped, plucked, hanky, whirled*

1. Read the story through one time without interruptions to provide a context for the new words. My students began to make guesses about which words they thought would be selected for the game. There is no question they were listening for new words as I read!

2. Give each child a set of index cards and ask students to write each word on a separate card. You can write the words on the board for them to copy, but I prefer to dictate the words and spellings. That way, as the students write, I can call their attention to the meaning as the word appeared in the story. These cards are saved and used for Line It Up activities throughout the week. I had my students keep their cards in a small plastic bag in their desks.

3. Have the students mix up the cards. Read the story again, interjecting a short definition of each target word when it appears in the text. As students hear the target words, they line up the cards on the desks. When all words have been placed in line, a student calls off the list to check.

Day 2—Provide meaning clues.

1. In the first position, place the word that means "to be pleased or satisfied." (Students slide the card with the word *content* to the top left corner of the desk.)

2. In the second spot, place the word that means "to have grabbed something quickly." (The card with *snatched* is placed to the right of *content*.)

3. Continue providing clues until all words are placed in line.

4. Check by having a student call off the words, and review the meaning clues to verify.

Day 3—Provide structural clues to draw students' attention to spelling, prefixes, and suffixes.

1. In the first position, place the word that is past tense, but does not use the *-ed* ending. (*swept*)

2. In the second position, place the word that needed its final consonant doubled before adding *-ed*. (*whipped*)

3. Continue until all words have been placed.

Day 4—Use meaning clues again, but this time emphasize synonyms, antonyms, or usage.

1. In the first spot, place the word that means the same thing as *picked*. (*plucked*)

2. In the second position, put the word that is a synonym for *spin*. (*whirled*)

3. In the third spot, place the word that would be an antonym, or opposite, for *unhappy*. (*content*)

4. Continue until all cards have been placed.

Day 5—Spelling and/or phonemic awareness clues can be given.

1. In the first spot, put the word that rhymes with *panky*. (*hanky*)

2. Next, place the word that has the /ch/ sound in the middle. (*snatched*)

3. Continue until all cards have been placed.

The words you have selected, along with the particular skills your students need to practice, will guide your choices. You may play Line It Up daily, or just a few times a week. Each time you play, your students learn a little bit more about the words. When students call off the words to check their responses, they are hearing and reading the words. You can quickly check for understanding as well.

Teacher: Yes, *hanky* goes in the first spot. And what is a *hanky*?

Teacher: Correct! *Snatched* has the *-ed* suffix that sounds like a *t*. *Snatch* means to grab something quickly.

Act It Out

Most of us have played the game charades at some time. Successfully acting out a word requires the actor to know quite a bit about its meaning. The student must think of a definition for the word, and then put it in a context that can be visualized. The rest of the class must use the clues provided to determine what action they are seeing.

When your target list includes a lot of verbs, this activity can help your students see and feel the differences between similar terms, such as *step* and *stomp*, or *hop* and *leap*.

It is great to use Act It Out during those times when your class needs something to get the wiggles out. Those underutilized moments just before lunch or dismissal can become a vocabulary review, maximizing your instructional time every day.

For instance, you might read a short book that contains examples of vivid verbs. *Worms Wiggle* by David Pelham (1989) is a good example. During transition times, you can review word meanings as you wait for the bell. The final game can be played at the end of the week when you have a longer period of time.

1. Discuss the meanings of the verbs contained in the text, such as *wiggle, pounce,* and *glide*.

2. As a group, agree on appropriate ways to demonstrate those movements.

3. Select students to act out the verb of their choice. The remaining students guess which word they have chosen.

Picture It

Word posters (Tompkins, 2006) help students develop a visual image related to word meaning. In this activity, students usually write the word being studied on a small poster. Students then draw a picture that illustrates the word's meaning and write a sentence using the word.

Visualization is a powerful strategy to use, but my students often had difficulty thinking of how to illustrate the words. To help them, I created Picture It cards. These cards might include an illustration, but since I am certainly not an artist, they often consisted of the word written in a way that illustrates its meaning. For example, the word *shimmering* would be written in large letters covered with glitter. *Sprint* would be written at an angle, with little lines drawn to indicate fast movement. The students enjoyed making their own Picture It cards in centers. Often, they just copied my samples, but some students embellished the pictures in creative ways. The clues provided by the illustrations would be reviewed in the Line It Up activity on a subsequent day.

Another variation of this activity is to generate the illustrations as a class. For example, one of the words we encountered was *wander*. I explained to the children what the word meant, and then we had several volunteers *wander* around the classroom to demonstrate. How could we illustrate the word on our Picture It card in a way that would show us its meaning? As a class, we came up with the following card:

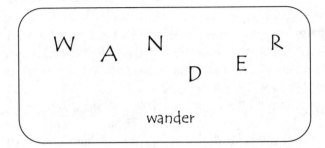

While the end result may not have been meaningful to others, it was very effective for these students because they were involved in the creation of the image. Wander actually became a favorite word and appeared frequently in students' writings.

Infusing the Language of Literacy

We have a tendency when we teach young children to simplify our language to make it easy for them to understand. Like many of you, I suspect, I used easy-to-understand terms, such as naming words, action words, and describing words when referring to nouns, verbs, and adjectives. But listening to a group of boys discussing dinosaurs, it occurred to me that a child who can say *Tyrannosaurus rex* can certainly learn the word *noun*. I found that my students really enjoyed learning words that surprised and amazed their parents. Some of them even got in the habit of asking other teachers if they knew what *macrons* and *breves* were. While my colleagues didn't exactly appreciate being shown up by first graders, it did encourage some students to continue learning new words to stump the teachers.

It is important to use the vocabulary of literacy when having discussions about stories and writing. Using the terms *character, setting, problem,* and *solution* as you talk about stories you are reading to the children is an important way of developing these concepts and enhancing their listening comprehension and future reading comprehension (Mountain, 2000).

Retelling stories is currently used to assess comprehension in young readers. Children have more complete and detailed retellings when they have had practice identifying key story elements and can use the vocabulary of literacy in their retellings.

Commercially prepared comprehension cards are available to help students identify story elements. Each child is given a pack of cards that contains generic terms for narrative text. The child uses the cards to learn to navigate the text, identify the important elements during reading, and as a guide in constructing a complete retelling. I really liked the idea of these cards, but found that the students who needed this support the most benefited little from the exercise. They would simply flip through the stack, not really knowing what they were looking for. Whole-group instruction in the language and use of the cards made a tremendous difference in my students' understanding of story elements and the retelling process. This is the procedure I follow:

1. Begin by placing word cards for story elements down the left side of the pocket chart.

2. As you place each card, discuss what the term means with your students and provide examples from familiar stories.

3. Tell your students a familiar fairy tale. Stop frequently and ask your students questions such as:

   a. "Do we know who the characters are in the story?"

   b. "Have we learned what the setting of the story is—where the story takes place?"

4. When elements of the story have been identified, slide the card to the right of the pocket chart.

   a. "We have learned about the characters and the setting, but we still aren't sure about the problem. Listen to the next part and let's see if we can figure it out."

5. When you have finished telling the story, slide all of the cards back to the right side of the pocket chart.

6. Model retelling the story, sliding the cards over as you mention each element.

7. Repeat the process with unfamiliar stories on subsequent days.

When your students have developed proficiency with the task, provide each student with a set of element cards. As you read a story, the students slide the card to the right when they think they have learned about that element.

> "Johnny, I see you moved your *setting* card. Can you tell me what the setting of the story is?"

My students kept these cards on their desks while reading independently and then used the cards to be sure that their retellings were complete. This instructional sequence was very successful in helping my students both identify story elements and include those elements in their retellings.

Phonological and Phonemic Awareness

The research on phonological and phonemic awareness is clear. These skills are critical to the later development of efficient decoding skills and are strongly related to future reading success. But phonemic awareness can also affect the way that children are able to acquire new words from the stream of language around them. In fact, some of the most recent research shows a reciprocal relationship between vocabulary and phonemic awareness. The more words children know, the more fine-tuned their phonological awareness becomes (Metsala & Walley, 1998).

We may be tempted to take some aspects of phonological awareness for granted, such as separating the speech stream into words. These skills can present difficulties for our at-risk children, particularly the second-language learners.

One of my students was a newcomer from China. When she started school as a second grader, Jenny had only been in the United States for about three weeks. We were very fortunate to have a Mandarin-speaking teacher on our faculty in the ESL program. Jenny spent most of the language arts block with her and the remainder of the day in my regular second-grade classroom. Jenny listened and watched, working hard to make sense of the language around her. One day, Jenny asked the ESL teacher in Mandarin, "What is a *boyungol*?" The teacher, puzzled, asked her where she had heard the word. Jenny replied that the teacher was always saying *boyungol* to the class. When I said "Boys and girls, take out your books," Jenny heard one long word instead of three.

This student was trying hard to make sense of what she was hearing. She tried to use the context of the situation to help, but because she could not perceive the breaks in the speech stream and had difficulty identifying all the sounds, she was not able to determine what was being said.

It is not only children who are learning English who experience these difficulties. How many of us have asked young children to say, not sing the alphabet, and discover that *elemenopee* is all one word? Listening to children recite the Pledge of Allegiance always results in some interesting "new" words as well.

Some sounds are easily confused. Often, when talking on the phone, we have to clarify what we say—even when we are spelling. Is that *P* as in *Peter*, or *B* as in *Bob*? When a child hears a word that is not in his vocabulary, distinguishing between sounds is even more difficult.

During February in the Houston area, all thoughts turn to the Houston Livestock Show and Rodeo, one of the largest events of its kind. To establish the mood for the morning announcements, our principal played the song, "If You're Gonna Play in Texas (You Gotta Have a Fiddle in the Band)."

Children write words the way they hear them. One of my students scripted the following version in his journal: *If your gonna play in Texas, you gotta have a fiddo in a pan.* This entry came complete with an illustration of a small creature, presumably the fiddo, standing in a skillet.

As you plan lessons to develop your students' phonemic awareness, keep the partner objective of vocabulary in mind to get the most learning out of each activity.

The Bag Game

The Bag Game, developed by Lewkowicz (1994), is an example of an activity that can be used to develop phonemic awareness. For this activity, you need two bags or boxes, and several pairs of matching items, such as two socks, two crayons, two pencils, and two markers. Divide the items so that each bag has one item from each pair. Two children are chosen to play: one takes the role of the Sounder, and the other is the Matcher. The Sounder reaches into the bag and selects an item, but keeps it hidden from the class and the Matcher. The Sounder produces the initial phoneme for the item. The Matcher must then select the item from his bag that begins with the same initial phoneme and hold it up for the class to see. The class serves as the jury and decides if the match is correct.

Variations on the Bag Game

1. Play the game using ending sounds, medial vowels, or rhyming words. Most phonemic awareness skills would be appropriate for the game with a few adjustments to the procedures. For syllable matching, the Sounder could clap the number of syllables in the word, and the Matcher would find the item with the same number of syllables.

2. Infuse more complex vocabulary into the game. Instead of a pencil for the sound of /p/, find a small plastic penguin. Inexpensive bags of small plastic animals can be used. The items do not have to match if they have the same target phoneme. For example, you may pair the penguin and a pelican.

3. Once the class is familiar with the game, place it in a center to provide extra practice for students.

I Spy

This familiar game can be used in a variety of ways to develop both phonemic awareness and vocabulary. We usually play the game by selecting objects that are visible in the room. The teacher starts the game and establishes the pattern to follow.

- "I spy something that rhymes with *sock*." (*clock*)
- "I spy something that ends with /k/." (*desk*)

In many cases, you will need to provide additional clues to rule out multiple possibilities. Or you can simply accept the choice as correct even if that was not the answer you had in mind!

To increase the vocabulary power of the game, consider using photographs in the pocket chart, or small items such as plastic animals on a tray or the chalk ledge. For example, you might have a giraffe, hippopotamus, lion, and monkey on the tray and say, "I spy an animal that has five syllables."

Bingo: Infusion Style

Bingo can be played to teach a variety of phonological and phonemic awareness skills. This easy-to-make version of the game can be used to expose children to new vocabulary. You can have blank bingo cards made and laminated, but I found that my students enjoyed just making their own. Simply fold a sheet of 8½" x 11" copy paper into eight squares. Students can fill in the spaces to match the focus of the game.

1. **Sounds Bingo:** Students select letters and write one in each square. At times, you may want to limit the students in their choices to focus on a particular group of sounds. For example, if you are focusing on short vowel sounds, you would limit your students to writing those letters. As the teacher calls out the word, the student must isolate and identify the initial sound. If that letter is on the student's bingo card, he or she can cover it with a marker. Covering one row of four results in a bingo for that child.

2. **Themed Bingo:** Selecting a category for your bingo words provides a semantic link for the students as they hear new words. They may be unfamiliar with the specific word but understand that it is an animal name. Try using more uncommon animal words, such as *walrus, seal, orangutan, jaguar,* or *cobra*, instead of *cat* and *dog*. This activity is more effective if you can obtain a deck of animal cards. You can also pull pictures off the Internet to show what these animals look like as you say their names. There are themed lists in Appendix A to get you started, or you can look to the many published alphabet books for additional sources of words.

Phonics and Spelling

Phonics and spelling are important components of the primary curriculum. They provide foundational skills for the decoding and encoding that support the development of word recognition and word-identification strategies. Many teachers find that using a particular series or program is useful in ensuring that lessons are presented in a systematic way. It is a simple matter to infuse a little vocabulary and get the most out of these instructional moments.

Making Words

Making Words (Cunningham, 2000) is widely used in primary classrooms to develop the alphabetic principle and phonics skills in a hands-on manner. There are many collections of making words activities available, but you can also script your own. While the focus of your instruction needs to remain on the spelling patterns, it is easy to infuse a little vocabulary instruction into the mix as well. Cunningham, Moore, Cunningham, and Moore (2004) suggest using a word from a topic the class is currently studying for the mystery word. You could also select a word from one of your class collections. For example, in a unit on butterflies, you might select the word *chrysalis* and develop a Making Words lesson similar to this sample.

Letters needed: *a, i, c, h, r, y, s, s, l*

- "Take two letters and make *is*. It *is* freezing outside this morning."
- "Now change a letter and make *as*. Your hands are *as* cold as ice."
- "Add a letter to make *has*. It *has* just started to sleet."
- "Let's start with a new three-letter word, *ail*. The word *ail* is a synonym for *sick*."
- "Add a letter to make *sail*. The ship set *sail* at noon."
- "Now change a letter to make *hail*. The *hail* pellets were as big as grapes during the thunderstorm."
- "Change a letter to make *rail*. The circus traveled by *rail*, by train, to the next city."
- "Take away a letter and change a letter to make *air*. Oxygen is in the *air* we breathe."
- "Add a letter to make *lair*. The panther slept in its *lair*, or den."
- "Change the beginning of the word to make *chair*. The king sat in a big fancy *chair* called a throne."
- "Take away a letter to make *char*. I *char* the meat on the grill."
- "Now, use all of the letters to make the secret word. Here's a clue— it is part of the life cycle of the butterfly."

The basic structure and sequence of the lesson is unchanged, but vocabulary is infused in three ways. First, words likely to be unknown to the students, such as *ail, lair,* and *char,* are deliberately incorporated into the lesson. The accompanying sentence uses the word in a simple context that supports definitional learning. Second, for familiar words such as *sail, rail,* and *chair,* the sample sentences present the words in a new context. In the case of *chair,* a familiar concept is used to develop the new word *throne.* Finally, a few opportunities for figurative language can be seen in this example. Familiarity with these common patterns of language will help your students as they encounter similes, metaphors, and idioms in their reading and use them in their writing.

Spelling

If your district encourages or requires you to use a basal series for spelling, you can still infuse some vocabulary into this highly structured context. It will take some searching, but you can find unusual words to fit many of the typical spelling patterns found in basal spellers. As you develop your students' understanding of the pattern through the week, you will have countless opportunities to review the meanings and uses of the words. For example, in a unit featuring the *ing* and *ink* phonograms, you could add the animals *mink* and *skink.* The word *sum* would fit easily into a spelling unit on short vowels. Although it is a simple word to spell, it represents an important math concept. On your weekly test, your sentence might be something like, *Sum*—the answer to an addition problem is called the *sum.*

You may not want to include the words on your weekly test, but if you have application, extension, or enrichment activities built into your instructional design, novel vocabulary words are a natural.

Writing

When your students begin to spontaneously use infusion words in their writing, it is a cause for celebration. Whether in the context of a writing workshop, journal writing, or informal notes, we can feel confident that our students' vocabularies are growing when the words we have introduced begin to appear in written form. For some children, infusion words will pop up early and often. For others, you will need to structure lessons that encourage such risk taking.

Children often approach writing tasks with dread. They limit what they write to what they think they can complete quickly and with minimal revisions. Instead of risking the use of a novel vocabulary word, they will stick with the tried and true. In order to get our students to branch out, we need to establish a climate in our classrooms that supports their efforts by providing sufficient modeling, as well as opportunities to share and revise their work.

Model the Use of Vocabulary

Mini-lessons, conducted during the course of writer's workshop, are an effective vehicle for developing students' writing skills. As you model your writing strategies, don't forget to infuse vocabulary. Show your students how word choice can make the difference between an acceptable composition and an exceptional one.

Script a short passage as an illustration:

"Last weekend, I went to the beach with my family. We had a good time."

Teacher: "Boys and girls, I am not happy with the word *good* because it really doesn't describe my time at the beach very well. Let me tell you a little more and you help me think of a better word than *good*. Maybe one of the words from our Amazing Adjectives collection will help."

After the students have completed their drafts, they can work in pairs to try to find places where a better word choice could be made. You can target specific word types. For example, you might ask the children to be sure to include at least two vivid verbs or descriptive words in their stories.

Model the Use of Infusion Words

Some students will need your help to incorporate infusion words into their writing. As you conference with students, point out places where words they have experienced in other contexts might strengthen their writing.

In writing about strawberries, Ashley (age 7) used the ubiquitous adjective *good*. As I talked with her about her work, I explained that I really couldn't tell from the word *good* whether she liked strawberries a lot, or just a little. Ashley stated that she liked strawberries a lot—they were her favorite fruit. "Can you think of a word you have heard in the cafeteria that would tell me that?" Ashley's final composition included this sentence:

Strawberrys are delicious.

Although it isn't much of a difference, it was enough to get Ashley thinking more about her choice of words and encouraged her to use words that she had heard, but was afraid to try to spell.

With your support, your students will work to find just the right word to express their thoughts. After an encounter with a snake on the way to our classroom, Sara (age 8) wrote, "One day on the way to ESL we saw a snake by the door. It was so discusthing!" There was little doubt how this student feels about snakes!

Jeremy (age 6) writes a description of a banana that paints a vivid picture of the shape and texture of his favorite fruit:

> *A banana is skinny and long and shaped like a cresent moon.*
> *It feells soft and squishy in your mouth.*

Celebrate the Fearless Use of Rare Words

Another way to promote the use of uncommon words is to encourage your students to write about what they know. Whether it is playing a video game, a sport, or camping, most children feel that they are pretty good at something. Think about the students in your class. Chances are you already know what they are interested in. With a little infusion magic on your part, you will have a panel of experts. Every year, I seemed to have at least one resident expert in paleontology, who dazzled the class with his knowledge of dinosaurs. The child who spends the weekend watching his older brothers play sports can become the class expert in soccer, baseball, or football.

One young baseball enthusiast was totally absorbed in the home run derby that went on during 1999 between Mark McGwire and Sammy Sosa. He reported regularly to the class on the battle for the record. His journals were full of batting averages, RBIs, ERAs, and play-by-play descriptions of the baseball games he had watched that week.

As your students write, encourage them to share their expert knowledge and incorporate the specialized vocabulary of the field. If you establish a climate of acceptance for less-than-conventional spellings and occasional inaccuracies, your students will feel free to take risks. For example, look at the use of specialized vocabulary by Erika, writing to her first-grade class about her skill in ballet, a field dominated by French terms.

> *Hi! My name is Erika and I'm really good at ballet because my ballet teacher says that I am the best in my whole bellat [ballet] class. Air-a-bes-so-ta [arabesque sautee] is the move I like best. A-bruch-so-ta [I never could figure this one out] is the hardest move in ballet. Que-pay [coupee] is another hard one.*
>
> *I'm really good. Shantoma [changement] is a kind of jump. How I love ballet. Gomb-bomb-mommies [grande battement] are something hard to explain.*
>
> *4th pourshin [position] is a leg stretch to stretch ones legs. Gomg-bomb-momies-qupay leeddy-foot quenasa-qu-pay are all in leg streach.*
>
> *That's what I'm good at!*

Erika assumed the role of expert as she described the steps she learned in her ballet class. She tackled the spelling of some very difficult French words, applying her developing knowledge of English spelling patterns. Although I don't know exactly what some of the words are that she tried to write, she was not afraid to use the vocabulary she was learning in her writing.

Brainstorming

Brainstorming is a great way to get your students to be fast thinkers and writers. In brainstorming, students are given a short period of time to generate a list of as many words as they can that fit a specified category. I usually give my students two minutes, but you can adjust the time to meet the needs of your students. Spelling is not a concern in this fast-paced activity.

1. Introduce the topic: Give your students a brief explanation of the topic or category for the brainstorm, along with two or three examples. This gets their brains in gear.

2. At the signal (I used a bell) everyone begins to write. The goal is to think of as many words as possible.

3. At the end of two minutes, signaled again by the bell, everyone stops writing, counts their entries, and writes that number at the top of their papers.

4. The student who has the most entries reads his list to the class. The class has two tasks during this time. First, students listen to be sure that all of the words belong in the category. Then they check their lists and mark the words that are read.

5. After the list has been read, other students may add words that appeared on their lists. By doing this, even the child who wrote only a few words has the opportunity to make a contribution. Some students will try very hard to think of a word that no one else will have!

When you first begin to use brainstorms, start with very broad categories, for example, animal names, items in the classroom, or colors. As your students develop their writing and vocabulary, narrow the categories. For example, you might have them brainstorm vivid verbs or adjectives. During a science or social studies unit on natural resources, you might do a brainstorm on uses of water.

For younger students, the process is essentially the same, but the teacher serves as scribe. If you are fortunate enough to have an instructional aide in your class, you can divide the class into two groups and have each group generate its own list. If you do this as a whole-class activity, give the children time to think of their responses, and then allow each child to contribute to the class list. Lists generated in brainstorming sessions can be used for other sorting and categorizing activities, or posted as word collections.

Conclusion

Vocabulary instruction does not need to be dull and lifeless. With some planning and a little imagination, you can infuse vocabulary into your reading and writing instruction in a way that develops expressive language skills and ultimately improves reading and writing abilities. Vocabulary becomes something your class looks forward to as you weave new words into your literacy instruction. I think you will be amazed at what a little infusion will do!

CHAPTER 6

Extending Infusion Into the Content Areas

The vocabulary demands of the content areas present many challenges to young learners. In fact, the lack of content-specific vocabulary is often cited as a leading cause of the fourth-grade slump, a drop in reading achievement scores that often occurs between the third and fourth grades (Hirsch, 2003).

Although many factors contribute to the problem, three areas stand out: a lack of background knowledge, the abstract nature of the concepts represented, and morphemic complexity.

Experiences that students have outside of school can enhance the development of content vocabulary. It is just common sense that students who have been to a natural history museum and have seen the skeletons of dinosaurs will have a different level of understanding when reading or hearing about dinosaurs than students who have only heard descriptions or viewed pictures in books. As they encounter new words and concepts in books and in classroom discussions, they have an existing schema, or framework, that can be used to sort and categorize this new information.

Students who have not had this outside experience are building their schemas from the ground up. They are already behind before they have started. These students will need more scaffolding and more frequent exposure to vocabulary and concepts to aid their comprehension of classroom instruction.

Many students struggle with vocabulary in the content areas because it often represents abstract concepts. We can't just show a picture of freedom—we have to build students' understanding through discussion and examples. Additionally, these concepts are essential to the content, not just peripheral. A student who doesn't quite understand the word *hanky* in Pat Hutchins's *The Wind Blew* can still understand and enjoy the text. In contrast, consider this excerpt from a social studies leveled reader:

- Good citizens play fair.
- Good citizens share.
- Good citizens obey laws.

With this text, taken from *Be a Good Citizen* by Bonita Ferraro (2003), a child who does not understand what a citizen is will not understand it. Just think about the complex and abstract vocabulary found in the patriotic songs we teach our children. Haven't you had students who think *tisofthee* is a word, as in "My country *tisofthee*?" Most young children recite the Pledge of Allegiance with little understanding of the complex concepts of republic, nation, liberty, and justice. In fact, listening to what they are really saying can be very entertaining.

Difficulties also arise as we consider that concepts such as fairness and responsibility, both objectives in many primary social studies curricula, are socially constructed. What is fair to you may not seem fair to the student.

A third factor is that many of these content words are morphemically complex—longer words with more prefixes and suffixes attached, often based on Latin or Greek roots that are less familiar to children. Teaching our students to notice the parts of words that are the same and to hear the root word in longer, more complex words will help them build the foundation they need to tackle the multisyllabic words of content vocabulary.

While content vocabulary is often considered the work of the upper elementary teachers, we need to begin building these stores of knowledge in our youngest learners. Many of the strategies typically used with older students can be redesigned to be developmentally appropriate for young children. For this chapter, we focus on three broad categories of activities that support the learning of content vocabulary: visualization, making connections, and morphemic analysis.

Can You See It?
Using Visualization Strategies

Visual imagery is a powerful tool for helping young children to learn the meanings of unfamiliar words. Visualization can be developed through a variety of instructional strategies. Photographs, videos, and realia can support learning in a language-free context. Graphic organizers can be used to help children see how ideas and concepts are related. Manipulatives and physical activity get children actively engaged in the visualization process.

Young children learn so much by touching and feeling—seeing the real item rather than just a picture. Looking through a telescope will mean so much more to your students than just listening to you describe how it works. Before reading the folk tale "The Great Enormous Turnip" with my class, I brought in a large turnip for my children to examine. They had a better understanding of the exaggeration in the story after seeing and feeling the uncommon vegetable.

Photographs, illustrations, and videos can be helpful in building background knowledge quickly, and in a way that minimizes the dependency on language. Children can watch a video on the rain forest and develop a picture in their mind that will support your explanation of the forest layers. They can study the beautiful and detailed illustrations by Laura Regan in Jane Yolen's *Welcome to the Green House* (1993).

Visualization involves more than just pictures. Graphic organizers help children see the relationships between words. Manipulatives can be used in a variety of ways that help children get a picture in their minds of what abstract concepts mean. Physical activity provides another avenue to visualization as children see and experience word meanings. The activities that follow demonstrate some of the ways that visualization can be used to support vocabulary development.

Graphic Organizers

Graphic organizers can be used in a variety of ways to help children visualize the connections between words as well as to develop their understanding of concepts and meanings. Many Internet and text-based sources can help you find graphic organizers that will best match your instruction. As students utilize the organizers, they engage with vocabulary in an active manner. The end product provides them with a visual summary of their thinking.

Students can take an organizer with the title filled in and be sent to search through books on the rain forest for the names of animals. Students who have used a web like the one on the following page may not remember exactly what a tapir is, but they are likely to remember that it is associated with the rain forest.

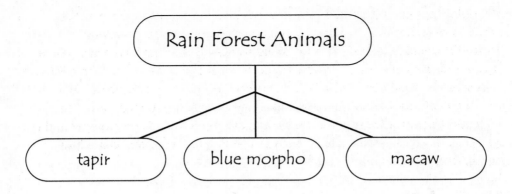

Triple Play

The Triple Play activity uses a simple three-column graphic organizer to help students think about the differences between words. The activity, described in detail in Chapter 3, can readily be adapted for content-area vocabulary and concepts. For example, give the students a list of math terms to write in the center column. Their task is to find a related term that would represent a lesser quantity, time period, or amount for the left column, and a term for a larger amount in the right column. Some children may require the additional support of having all three words provided, so all they need to do is place them in the correct columns. Other children can generate their own words for the right and left columns. At times, you may want the students to search through their textbook or other nonfiction books for the answers.

Triple Plays are useful for reviewing difficult concepts. Children who have worked hard to master time, measurement, capacity, and money will benefit from activities like Triple Plays that keep the skills fresh in their minds.

Consider the following example:

−		+
second	minute	hour
week	month	year
triangle	rectangle	pentagon
penny	nickel	dime
one	hundred	thousand

Triple Plays can be created to review science and social studies content words as well. Terms such as *city, state, country,* or *mayor, governor, president* would be appropriate for social studies. Reviewing landforms (*plain, hill, mountain*) or bodies of water (*lake, sea, ocean*) is easy with Triple Plays.

A science Triple Play might include *breeze, wind, gale,* or *drizzle, rain, downpour* after a weather unit. During a unit on space, you might give the students the word *planet* in the center and ask them to find something found in space that is bigger than a planet, such as the *sun* or a *star*, and something smaller such as a *moon* or an *asteroid*.

Manipulatives

Using manipulatives supports the active construction of meaning. We typically think of using manipulatives in math to help students move from concrete to abstract thinking, such as in teaching addition and subtraction, but they can be used in learning a variety of content vocabulary. In the following activities, manipulatives support the development of concepts in science and math.

See the Difference

Hands-on experiences are a critical component of young children's learning. While we usually start with the words when we teach vocabulary, this activity gets the children involved in describing the differences between objects. Once they have the concept in mind, attaching a label to it is a simple matter.

For example, you may give children small samples of wax paper, plastic wrap, and cardboard. Ask them to look at a light through each sample and describe the differences between them. As children discuss the way that they can see clearly through the plastic wrap, introduce the word *transparent*. When they talk about the wax paper, tell them it is *translucent*. You can see some light through it, but things are cloudy or fuzzy. Finally, teach them the word *opaque* to describe what happens with the cardboard: no light can pass through. As an extension, generate a list of other things that are transparent, translucent, and opaque.

You can use the same process with texture words. Give students a tiny amount of contrasting substances, such as powdered sugar and granular sugar. Have them rub a bit between their thumb and finger and describe the difference in the way the two sugars feel. Introduce the words *gritty* and *powdery* to describe those textures. Find other items with similar textures for students to sort, or you can brainstorm a list of items as a class.

Math Concepts

Manipulating materials is a powerful way of helping students to visualize abstract math concepts, but manipulatives are not just for calculations in math. Because math concepts such as greater than, less than, equal to, decrease, increase, symmetry, even, and odd can be represented by arranging and rearranging groups of objects, students can be given edible items such as cereal, small cookies, or candies to work with. Reusable cubes, counters, or paper shapes can also be used, or students themselves can become the manipulatives.

Sample Script

1. Give each student a baggie with 20 cubes, candies, cereal, or similar items.

2. "Boys and girls, I want you to start off by dividing your cubes into two equal piles."

3. "Take three cubes from the pile on the left and add them to the group on the right."

4. "Now the pile on the right is greater than the pile on the left."

5. "Subtract five cubes from the pile on the right and add them to the pile on the left."

6. "Now the pile on the right is less than the pile on the left."

7. "Decrease the left pile and increase the right pile so that they are both equal again."

8. "Create a design with your cubes that has symmetry."

This type of exchange can be done very quickly as a warm-up before students begin work on their math lesson for the day. Follow each step or direction with a restatement of the concept, preferably by the students. For example, after Step 2, ask a student to tell you what the word *equal* means. Or you might ask the students to count the number in each pile. "You have 10 cubes in each pile, so they are . . ." The students will supply the word *equal*.

These same routines can be repeated using the children as manipulatives. Divide the class into two equal groups: "What do we need to do to make this group greater than the other group?"

Play Clay

Homemade or purchased play clay is great fun for children to use as they develop concepts of measurement. Have the students make two snakes from the clay.

Teacher: "Boys and girls, can you make one snake longer than the other?"

Student: "Stretch out one snake."

Teacher: "Mary, can you tell me about your snakes?"

Student: "This snake is longer than that one"

Teacher: "Now make the snakes equal in length again. This time, can you make two snakes that are equal in length, but make one wider than the other?"

Physical Activity and Visualization

Take it outside and get your students physically involved. To teach the concept of symmetry, divide your students into pairs. Have the pairs stand along a line—the line of symmetry—and decide how to stand so that they demonstrate symmetry along that line. Infuse recess games such as Mother May I? with math concepts:

"Mother says you may take more than six, but fewer than eight steps."

Other activities, such as bouncing a ball, jumping rope, and hopping can be used in much the same way. For example, while on the playground, ask one student to bounce a ball five times. Ask the next student to bounce the ball two fewer times. The next child can bounce it the number that represents the value of a dime. The same type of activity can be done with hopping or jumping rope.

Making It Fit: Finding Connections

Vocabulary development increases when students learn to make connections between words and ideas and their existing knowledge (Greenwood, 2002). Semantic mapping, categorization, and sorting are commonly used strategies to help students understand novel content vocabulary. These activities require the students to think about similarities and differences between words. Concept Circles and Clothesline are two easy-to-use activities that help students make those important semantic connections.

Concept Circles

Concept Circles (Harmon, Wood, & Hedrick, 2006) are an extension of the categorization process described in Chapter 2. They help students visualize the relationships between content-area vocabulary words. A circle is drawn on the board and divided into fourths. Each section of the circle is programmed with a term. Three of the terms should be related in some way, and the fourth is unrelated.

The student's task is to shade the portion of the circle containing the term that does not belong, and then to identify the category to which the remaining words belong. For example, if the circle was programmed with the words *winter, spring, summer,* and *October,* students would identify the category as *seasons* and shade the section with the word *October,* since it names a month and not a season.

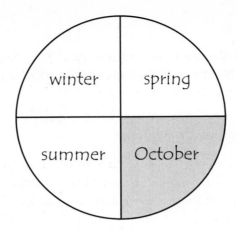

There are many adaptations that can be made to this activity to make it more interactive.

1. The circles can be cut out of paper and laminated, then put in a center for independent practice.

2. The circles can be cut out and each child can be given a section of the circle. Students move about the room to locate and join up with the remaining pieces of his or her circle.

3. Possible categories: the student can be given a section of the circle and asked to brainstorm possible categories.

4. What's my category? The teacher can supply one section of the circle each day, with students revising and refining their hypotheses as additional sections are revealed.

Clothesline

The Clothesline activity is an adaptation of Word Chains (Tompkins, 2006). Words can be drawn from any content area. In this activity, students sequence words according to a predetermined criterion, such as length of time, largest to smallest, least to greatest, or by order of occurrence. It is a great activity to use to help students think about shades of meaning between similar terms.

1. Select five to seven related terms. For example, in a social studies unit on geography, you might select words related to bodies of water: *puddle, pond, lake, sea,* or *ocean.*

2. Have students come up and hold up the cards so the words are visible to the class. Be sure the cards are in random order.

3. Select a student to arrange the cards (and a student to hold them). In this example, you might specify that they should be arranged from smallest to largest.

4. The class discusses any differences of opinion and resolves them.

5. In many cases, the cards can be rearranged by a different criterion. You can scramble the children again and ask a different student to arrange them from largest to smallest.

6. The terms you select will determine the variety of ways you can arrange and rearrange the cards.

Variations of the Clothesline can be made to suit your instructional purpose, and also the nature of the words selected. It can be done as a whole class as previously described, in small groups, or individually. Consider the following example for a group activity.

1. Divide the class into groups of five.

2. Each child has an index card. "Write an animal name on the front of your index card. You may write any animal you would like to, but it must be different from anyone else's in your group."

3. On the back of the card, each student writes a word that describes the way that animal moves: "Flip your card over to the back. Write the words that best describe the way that animal moves."

4. "Now, put yourselves in order from the smallest to the largest animal."

5. Each group explains to the class why they made its decisions. The conversation can get quite heated: "Do we mean *tall* or *large*?"

6. "Now put yourselves in order from the fastest to the slowest animal. If these animals were in a race, who would win?"

7. "Now flip your cards over to the side where you wrote the word describing how the animal moves. Are you still satisfied that they are in the correct order?"

The discussions that accompany this activity are lively, as children talk about how fast the hummingbird's wings flutter compared to the speed the penguin swims. The purpose of the activity is not to arrive at a definitive answer, but to engage students in thinking about the word meanings.

An additional variation of this activity has you build the chain from the students' responses, rather than having a predetermined set of words.

1. Select one student to start the chain.

2. Ask the student to name an animal. Write the selection on a card and have him or her stand at the front of the room.

3. The next student thinks of another animal and you write the response on a card.

4. "Is your animal larger or smaller than _____?" The student then stands at the right or left, depending on the size of the animal compared to the previous one.

5. Continue the process with additional students. As each student selects an animal, he or she determines where in the line to stand (with the help of the remaining students).

6. The chain can continue to include the entire class, or you can stop at any point. Hint: Have the students with the most extensive vocabularies go later in the cycle.

7. Once your chain has been constructed, you can have the students rearrange themselves according to a new criterion.

Although I initially introduced the sets of words in a large-group activity, card sets were then placed in a center. In the corner of the room I strung a piece of heavy string to serve as our clothesline. Previously taught word sets sat in a basket along with a supply of clothespins. Students worked individually or in pairs to place the words along the clothesline in the correct order. Have your students record their work on paper to monitor their progress.

Word lists for Clothesline activities can be taken from any of the content areas. For example, if you are studying weather, you could include words for wind, temperature, or precipitation.

> *breeze, wind, gale, hurricane*
>
> *cold, chilly, cool, warm, hot*
>
> *mist, drizzle, rain, downpour*

Social studies terms might include the seasons, days of the week, months of the year, or terms related to geography or government.

> *puddle, pond, lake, sea, ocean*
>
> *neighborhood, town, state, nation, continent*

It is easy to find math concepts for Clothesline activities. Place value terms, times, coin values, and geometric shapes can all be reviewed this way.

> *ones, tens, hundreds, thousands, millions*
>
> *triangle, rectangle, pentagon, hexagon*
>
> *second, minute, day, week, month, year*
>
> *penny, nickel, dime, quarter, half-dollar*

Building Blocks to Bigger Words: Morphemic Analysis

Even very young children develop an understanding of the way words are expanded through affixes. Children can begin to experience the way we use prefixes and suffixes to form new words. They can begin to identify the common root in words like *spectacles* and *spectator* and understand that both words relate to seeing.

Word trees are graphic organizers used to demonstrate the relationship between root words and derivatives. This version of the Word Tree activity has been adapted from the work of Kyleen Beers (2002).

Draw a simple outline of a tree on chart paper, chalkboard, or overhead projector. On the trunk of the tree, write the featured root word and a child-friendly definition. In the branches of the tree, write words that come from that root. Include a definition or a sample sentence.

For example, in math you might start with the root *cent* and explain that it means hundred. In the branches, write words such as *centigrade, centipede, century,* and *percent*. A unit on weather might include a Word Tree for the root word *meter* and include the words *altimeter, barometer, thermometer, hygrometer,* and *anemometer* in the branches.

Word Trees constructed on chart paper can be displayed on the walls of the classroom. Place a basket of die-cut leaf shapes in the library corner. As students encounter additional words with the focus root during independent reading, they can easily be added by drawing more branches on the tree. Students copy the sentence that contains the word on a leaf, and attach it to the branch as an example of how the word in used in context and to provide clues to its meaning.

Other Activities to Promote Morphemic Analysis

Word sorts are commonly used to group words by meaning or spelling pattern, but this activity can also be used to group words structurally. Sorting words by roots, prefixes, or suffixes helps students attend to key parts of longer words.

Graphic organizers can be used to help children see how big words are built from smaller words.

More Activities to Teach Content-Area Vocabulary

The remaining activities are easily adapted to give your students repeated exposure to content-area vocabulary and concepts in a fun way.

Linking Letters

This variation of the Word Chains activity will have your students scouring nonfiction texts and reference books! The object is to build the longest word chain possible with words that are related to the stated theme. For example, you might build a word chain of nouns, verbs, or adjectives. Or you might select a particular class of nouns, such as animals. You can select themes derived from your units of study, or your students might build a word chain for your school's home state during a social studies unit, or for the weather during science.

1. Select a topic.

2. Divide the class into small groups of three to four students.

3. Each group brainstorms a list of words associated with the category to get started.

4. Each group selects a key word to start off its chain.

5. The last letter of the key word determines the starting letter of the next word. For example, if the keyword Alamo is selected to start the Texas chain, the next word must begin with *o*.

6. Encourage students to use resource books to extend their chains.

7. As each group shares its chain, the students are responsible for explaining the terms and how they relate to the theme or topic.

In a unit dealing with animals, the students may generate the following list:

ape–elephant–turtle–eel–lion

A Texas chain might look like this:

Alamo–oil–Lubbock–King Ranch–Houston

A variation of this activity is to create a paper chain. Provide students with precut paper strips. As students locate words for their chain, they write each one, along with an appropriate illustration, on separate strips. The strips are then linked together to form a chain. There is always a competition to have the longest finished product.

Line It Up

This activity, also described in Chapter 5, provides opportunities for repeated exposure to content vocabulary in a variety of ways. By changing the nature of the clues, you can emphasize word meanings and even review phonological awareness and phonics patterns.

When beginning a unit, develop a list of the key vocabulary words. Students write the words on index cards, creating their own individual word sets. You can have them make all of the words at one time, but I preferred to start with five or six words and add to the stack as we encountered new important words.

For Line It Up, select five or six words from your list. Have your students take only those cards out of their sets, and lay them in random order along the bottom of their desks. Children listen to the clue, and slide the card they think matches that clue up into the appropriate position at the top of their desks. These clues may include definitions, synonyms, or antonyms. Change the clues, and you have a whole new game.

Sample Line It Up Lesson

This sample lesson, based on social studies content, will show you how easy it is to develop Line It Up lessons. One of the objectives common to our primary curriculum in Texas is for the students to understand the customs and history of national holidays.

Select five or six words that you want to emphasize. Choose words that you know from past experience represent difficult concepts for students, words that they will encounter in readings that you have planned, or words that are just fun to say. For this sample, I selected *Pilgrim, Plimoth, Mayflower, harvest, freedom,* and *cornucopia* from a unit on Thanksgiving. Script clues that will help your students connect the words to their meanings.

Meaning Clues

1. In the first position, put the word that means a horn-shaped basket filled with food. (*cornucopia*)

2. In the second position, place the word that names a group of people who left England to find a new home. (*Pilgrims*)

3. Next, place the word that means to gather the crops. (*harvest*)

4. In the fourth spot, put the ship that transported the Pilgrims from England to America. (*Mayflower*)

5. Next, when the Pilgrims landed and began to build their town, this is what they called it. (*Plimoth*)

6. In the last position is what the Pilgrims left England to get. (*freedom*)

Don't overlook opportunities to review these same words during other parts of your day. By changing the clues to focus on parts of speech, spelling patterns, or phonemic awareness, you can provide additional exposure to your content words while you review other literacy skills.

Phonological Awareness Clues

1. For the first word, if you take away the first sound of this word you are left with *arvest*. (*harvest*)

2. In the second spot, place the word that has five syllables. (*cornucopia*)

3. In the third position, put the word that has the /th/ sound at the end. (*Plimoth*)

4. Next, find the word that is a compound word. (*Mayflower*)

5. Finally, you should have a word left that has the same vowel sound in the first and second syllables. (*Pilgrims*)

6. The word that has the long *e* sound in the first syllable. (*freedom*)

Vocabulary 5 Ws

This activity helps to develop a depth of meaning that goes far beyond memorizing a definition. For a given vocabulary word, students need to find a *who, what, when, where,* and *why*. Who would use this item, or do this action? What is it? When would someone use the item or do the action? Where would they do this, or where would the item be found? And finally, why would this item be used, or this action done? Tailor the questions slightly to match the target word. For many words, an additional *how* question is also appropriate. How is this item done or used?

There are many graphic organizers available that can be used for the 5 Ws, or you can make your own. I had my students just trace their hands.

The following sample is based on a unit on space, showing the questions and possible answers students might generate.

- Target word: *astronomy*

- *Who* studies *astronomy*? A scientist who studies space is called an *astronomer*.

- *What* is *astronomy*? *Astronomy* is the study of space.

- *Where* would you study *astronomy*? You would study *astronomy* in an observatory.

- *When* is the best time to study *astronomy*? You need to study *astronomy* at night so you can see the stars and planets.

- *Why* do scientists study *astronomy*? Scientists study *astronomy* to learn more about the universe.

- *How* do *astronomers* study the stars? *Astronomers* use instruments, such as high powered telescopes, to study the stars.

Conclusion

In the primary grades, we typically focus our instruction on the very important work of teaching our students to read and write. Take a look at your lesson plans. You will likely see that the time allotted to language arts instruction far exceeds the amount of time for science and social studies. There is no question that teaching a balanced literacy program is a time-intensive proposition and there are only so many hours in the school day.

But we also know that our students need content-specific vocabulary if they are going to be successful in the upper grades. As the focus shifts from learning to read to reading to learn, they will encounter more and more unknown words that are content specific. The activities described in this chapter can help get your students off to good start by providing them with some strategies and building a core vocabulary of important concepts.

CHAPTER 7

Making Infusion Work for You

A Sample Unit

I have done it so many times. I read a great new instructional book or attend an innovative workshop, and I am so full of enthusiasm that I can't wait to get back into my classroom and put the things I have learned into practice.

But when I get back to school, and I am met with mountains of papers to grade, weekly folders to complete, parent phone calls to return, benchmark testing to conduct, and lesson plans to write, my resolve to try the new strategies falters. I have so much to do and it is so much faster to just continue with what I have been doing than to try to incorporate a new strategy.

"Next week," I tell myself, "I'll have more time to try something new." But there is never enough time for busy teachers. And so next week becomes next month. Next month becomes next year. The great new book goes on the shelf. The handouts from the workshop are filed away.

We know that in order for a word to become part of a learner's oral and reading vocabulary, there must be opportunities for authentic use structured into the daily experience. All of the vocabulary instruction we plan will be ineffective if we do not get our students using the words in their conversations and in their writing.

We are just like our students. We have to *use* our new learning for it to become a part of us. All the staff development in the world will not make a difference in our classrooms if we do not put the ideas into practice.

From Intentions to Implementation

Good intentions are not enough. Countless diets and exercise regimens fail because intention does not automatically lead to implementation. Getting started is often the hardest part. In the sections that follow, I will walk you through the creation of an infusion unit. Remember, infusion is a process, not a program. You decide what parts of the sample unit would be appropriate for your class. Start small. Try one or two activities at first. Add more as you gain confidence.

A Change in Thinking

Implementing infusion requires a change in the way we think about designing and writing lesson plans for literacy instruction. I have always had a problem with the term "balanced literacy." It conjures up the vision of a balance scale, the brightly colored plastic ones we use in our classrooms. A pile of little blocks of various weights sits to the side. The blocks are labeled with the identified components of early literacy: phonological awareness, alphabetic principle, fluency, vocabulary, and comprehension. The teacher carefully selects just enough of each component to "balance" her instruction.

I completely agree with the concept of balanced literacy, but an overemphasis on balance can result in modular instruction that is disjointed and low impact for the students. High-progress children seem to make intuitive connections. They recognize that the word they chanted and placed on the word wall that morning is the same word they just encountered in their reader. For our low-progress kids, these connections must be explicitly demonstrated and authentic uses for the skills must be shown.

Thinking of my literacy instruction as *integrated* rather than *balanced* helps me plan for those connections. My image of integrated literacy is a string of beads. The key components are present in various amounts, just as with balanced literacy. The key difference is the anchoring strand of instruction holding them all together. The strand provides a framework and structure that allows the students to see how the components of literacy are entwined.

Vocabulary can be one of the anchoring strands. Infusion threads vocabulary instruction through each component, creating a cohesive plan. By focusing on using vocabulary in multiple ways and contexts, children are provided with the best opportunities for taking ownership of the new words they are learning.

Rickards and Hawes (2007) share an example of this type of instruction in their description of a first-grade teacher who is focusing on the use of vivid verbs with her students. Students listened for these words during read-alouds, located them in their independent reading, and took ownership of them by using them in their writing. Instruction of this type will be far more effective in reaching the goal of the students assimilating the new words into their own vocabularies than the typical process of simply memorizing a list.

Getting Started: A Sample Unit

Vocabulary infusion starts with the words. The words you select for infusion can come from any number of sources, but children's literature is probably the best place to start. This sample unit demonstrates how you can take a piece of children's literature as the inspiration for infusion instruction. You can base a unit on a single text, or two or three texts that are similar in some way. The sample unit features two texts written and illustrated by Denise Fleming. *In the Small, Small Pond* and *In the Tall, Tall Grass* are complementary texts, similar in style and content, making them a good choice to combine in a unit of instruction. This particular unit is designed to take two weeks.

Selecting Texts for Infusion

The text you choose will shape the activities you design for the unit. The text will determine the words you choose for infusion, the length of the unit, and even the types of activities you select. Texts for infusion units should be selected on the basis of several criteria, many of which are the same ones you already use when choosing books to read aloud to your class.

First select texts with large, engaging illustrations. Since the illustrations are an important source of information about the vocabulary words, it is important that they be large enough for the children to see clearly.

Length is another consideration. Since you will be reading the text a number of times, shorter texts allow multiple readings to occur without a huge time investment. The brevity of the text allows you to keep the attention of your students as you elaborate on word meanings.

Most important, select texts that are full of interesting words. These words—what Beck, McKeown, and Kucan (2002) call Tier 2 words—are the type you will select for your infusion instruction.

The Fleming texts are infusion texts that focus on such concepts as wildlife in the pond and grass, topics that are familiar and interesting to most children. The colorful illustrations are highly supportive of the text. A big book is great if you have one, but large print and full-page illustrations make these books suitable for reading aloud in a whole-group context if a big book is not available. The rhythm and rhyme of the language are engaging enough to sustain children's interest through multiple readings of these texts, and they feature a good balance of familiar and novel words.

Analyzing the Text

Once you have selected the text(s), the next step in the process of developing an infusion unit is to analyze the vocabulary used in the text. The purpose of this analysis is to identify words to target for instruction. Create a list of possible words from the text, categorizing them by part of speech. Start with nouns and verbs with younger children. The nouns are usually represented in the illustrations in some way, and you can easily demonstrate most verbs yourself.

Once you have your list, sort the words into three categories. Group 1 contains the words that the children are likely to be familiar with. Group 2 consists of new words that represent familiar concepts, or familiar words that represent new concepts. The words that you think will be unfamiliar and represent new concepts go into Group 3.

Group 1 words will require little if any instruction. Most of your students will already know these words. Be cautious, however, in making assumptions about word knowledge. ESL students and children who have recently moved to your area often have different degrees of word knowledge.

Group 2 words require you to help students make the connections between the new term and the familiar concept. Your students may not have seen a *heron*, but they can relate it to the smaller *egret* they are familiar with. They may understand the word *sweep* as something you do with a broom, but not understand when it is used to describe the motion of a bat.

Group 3 words will need the most exposure. For these terms, your children will need to learn both the name and the concept. Of course, you will not expect the children to learn all of these terms. You select the ones that you feel will be best for your students to learn. You can always revisit the texts again at a later time and add more words!

Sample Unit Analysis

Since the texts I chose for my unit consist of nouns and verbs only, I began my analysis with the nouns. The texts contain illustrations of animals that are not specifically named, so I added them to my list.

In the Small, Small Pond

- Animals referred to by name: *tadpoles, geese, heron, minnow, whirligigs, swallows, muskrats*
- Animals pictured, but not named: *dragonfly, turtle, frog, crawfish, duck, raccoon*

In the Tall, Tall Grass

- Animals referred to by name: *caterpillars, hummingbirds, bees, ants, snakes, moles, beetles, fireflies, bats*
- Animals pictured but not named: *toads, rabbits*

Once my list was complete, I grouped the words into the three categories described above. While I felt that most students would be familiar with the unnamed animals, there were some I needed to think about. For example, in the Houston area, most children would be familiar with the crawfish depicted in *In the Small, Small Pond*. But growing up in suburban New Jersey, I had never seen a crawfish until I came to Texas and my son brought one home from the lake behind the house! Knowing the background of your students will allow you to prioritize words for instruction. The final grouping appears below.

Group 1	Group 2	Group 3
tadpole	heron	whirligig
turtle	swallow	muskrat
duck	minnow	dragonfly
frog	geese	hummingbird
crawfish	raccoon	fireflies
caterpillar	toads	moles
bats	beetles	
snakes		
bees		
ants		
rabbits		

You can follow the same process for the verbs found in the two texts.

In the Small, Small Pond

Verbs: *wiggle, jiggle, wriggle, waddle, wade, parade, hover, shiver, quiver, drowse, doze, close, lash, lunge, plunge, splitter, splatter, scatter, circle, swirl, twirl, sweep, swoop, scoop, click, clack, crack, dabble, dip, flip, splish, splash, flash, pile, pack, stack*

In the Tall, Tall Grass

Verbs: *crunch, munch, lunch, dart, dip, sip, strum, drum, hum, crack, snap, flap, pull, tug, lug, slip, slide, glide, ritch, ratch, scratch, skitter, scurry, hurry, zip, zap, snap, hip, hop, flop, stop, go, glow, lunge, loop, swoop*

After examining the vivid verbs found in the text, I again sorted them into three groups. As before, the first group included words that I thought would need little attention and instruction.

Group 1 might include: *wiggle, close, dip, pile, flap, flip, splash, pull, slide, hurry, hip, hop, sip, stop, go*

Group 2 words were likely to be familiar to the children, but in the text these familiar words carried new meanings. For example, a child may be familiar with the word *drum*, but not be sure of what it means in the context of the text: *Strum, drum, bees hum.*

Similarly, children are quite familiar with the word *lunch* when it is used as a noun, but in the following example, it is used as a verb. *Crunch, munch caterpillars lunch.*

Group 2 words might include: *crunch, munch, lunch, drum, hum, crack, snap, slip, zip, zap, sweep, parade, shiver, doze, splatter, circle, pack, stack, dabble, flash, scratch*

Group 3 words were those that I determined would be unfamiliar to most of the class and would require the most exposure in order for students to learn them.

Group 3 words might include: *jiggle, wriggle, waddle, wade, hover, drowse, lash, lunge, plunge, splitter, scatter, swirl, twirl, click, clack, dart, strum, tug, lug, glide, ritch, ratch, skitter, scurry, flop, glow, loop, swoop*

Narrowing Down the List

It is surprising how many novel words can be found in children's stories! There are far more of these words than it is possible to focus on for instruction.

Although you will expose your students to all of the words multiple times in the course of the infusion unit, you will want to narrow down the list to about ten words for special emphasis. My choices for this unit include the following verbs: *hover, waddle, swoop, flash, scurry, drowse, dart, scatter, lunge,* and *swirl.* The animal names identified for specific attention would include *heron, swallow, beetles, whirligigs, muskrats, moles, dragonflies, hummingbirds, fireflies,* and *minnow.*

Reading the Texts

During the course of the unit, you will read the text(s) several times. A variety of instructional strategies can make each reading a unique and enjoyable learning experience for your students. The specific text you choose for your infusion unit will determine the most appropriate types of activities to use in developing vocabulary. For example, some texts are rich in verbs, lending themselves to demonstration and physical activity, while others have more interesting nouns that can be pictured and labeled.

Initial Reading

The initial reading of the book consists of three parts: the introduction, the picture walk, and an uninterrupted reading. Before the first reading of the text, you will want to introduce the book as you do for any shared reading or read-aloud. Activating prior knowledge is always important before beginning a text.

The picture walk consists of talking your way through the pictures. Target words can be introduced by pointing at pictures, labeling, questioning, and discussion. This process is also very useful in verifying your previous analysis about which words the children already know. For example, in the Fleming text, I originally thought my students would not know what a heron was, but from my picture walk prior to reading, I found that many of them were already familiar with the word. After the introduction and picture walk, be sure to read the text through one time without interruption so children can enjoy the story.

Sample Unit Initial Reading

Teacher: "Boys and girls, today we are going to read a story about animals in the pond. Can anyone tell me what a pond is? What animals do you think we may find in this book? Let's take a picture walk and see if we are right."

As I turned the pages of the text, I identified animals that the children did not know by pointing and labeling.

Teacher: "This large bird is called a heron. These are tadpoles. Did you know that tadpoles are baby frogs? Here is a mother goose and her baby geese."

It was also important for me to identify the animals that are not named in the text as well, such as the dragonfly.

Teacher: "Look on this page. Do you see this large insect flying over the pond? This is a dragonfly."

After labeling the key animals in the picture walk, I read through the text without interruption so the students could experience the rich rhythm, rhyme, and sound of Fleming's story.

The Second Reading

The second reading of the text includes elaboration of word meanings. Elaboration provides information about target words with minimal disruption of the story. Elaboration can be nonverbal and consist of pointing to the illustration to indicate a specific item, or simple hand or facial gestures. The idea is to convey concise, child-friendly definitions of target words as you read. At first, you may find it helpful to use sticky notes to mark the places you want to insert comments and actions. The following sample will give you an idea of how easy it is. With practice, it will become a natural part of your reading routine.

Sample Unit Second Reading

These examples are drawn from *In the Tall, Tall Grass*.

Text: Pull, tug, ants lug

Teacher: (*make a pulling motion on the word* lug)

Text: Ritch, ratch, moles scratch

Teacher: (*point to the picture of the mole as you name it*)

Text: Crunch, munch, caterpillars lunch

Teacher: (*make chewing motion*)

Elaboration can also consist of labeling or a brief verbal explanation. For example, in the Fleming texts many of the animals are pictured, but not specifically mentioned in the text. In this case, I had a student I thought might not be familiar with the word toad, so I wanted to quickly identify the animal.

Text: Zip, zap, tongues snap

The illustration shows three toads catching flies, but the word *toad* does not appear on the page.

Teacher: "These are toads." (*points to the toads*)

Other words required a brief explanation.

Text: Slip, slide, snakes glide

Teacher: "*Glide* means that the snake moves smoothly and effortlessly through the grass."

Do not elaborate all your target words on every reading, but be sure that in the course of the unit you have given ample attention to all of the words.

Subsequent Readings

During the course of the two-week unit, you will read each text several times. Each reading has a slightly different focus of instruction. Many of the techniques you already use for shared reading can be adapted to include a vocabulary emphasis. For example, one reading may highlight the rich rhymes of the texts using a cloze technique. As you read the text to your students, pause before the last word of the page and allow students to generate the rhyme.

Teacher: "Wiggle, jiggle, tadpoles . . ."

Student: "Wriggle!"

Teacher: "Show me what it looks like when you wriggle."

Target words can be covered with sticky notes. Students make predictions about the word's identity and the word is revealed, letter by letter, to confirm their predictions. While the phonological-awareness skill of rhyming is the focus of the interaction, making a quick statement of the word's meaning, or having the students demonstrate the action as in the example above, adds a vocabulary dimension that reinforces the meanings of your target words.

Infusing Identified Vocabulary Into Your Daily Routines

Vocabulary during reading instruction is a standard part of most classrooms, but the real power of infusion lies in the way you incorporate vocabulary into the fabric of the classroom routines. Once you have identified the words you want to highlight for instruction, use your imagination and creativity to find unexpected places where you can plug them in. The activities described in previous chapters can be easily adapted to incorporate your target words. Some words work best with sorting activities; others can be worked into games on the playground. The following sample will demonstrate one way that target words can be reviewed in multiple settings throughout the day.

Sample Infusion Activities for the Fleming Unit

Classification

For these activities, I wrote words from the text on cards so they could be used for a variety of sorting activities. I used a pocket chart to introduce the activity to the students, and then placed it in a center for small-group work. For this unit, we sorted words on several days, each time by a different criterion.

Day 1—Sort animal names by fur, feathers, scales, or skin

Day 2—Sort animals by mammal, reptile, insect, amphibian

Day 3—Sort words into nouns and verbs

Day 4—Sort verbs by speed—"Is that motion fast, slow, or can it be both?"

Which One Does Not Belong?

For this activity, I provided four words and asked the students to identify which one did not belong in the group. Each day, as part of our morning work, I asked one group of students to explain their answers so I could be sure they understood the word meanings.

> *heron, swallow, muskrat, hummingbird*
>
> *circle, lunge, twirl, swirl*
>
> *flash, dart, zip, hover*
>
> *beetle, whirligig, hummingbird, firefly*

Analogies

In my class, we often practiced analogies as part of our calendar routine, but you can also write them on the board for seat work. The words for this unit worked well with analogies pairing animals and movements, animals with their habitats, and animals with their classifications.

1. *Heron* is to *lunge* as *dragonfly* is to _____.

2. *Toad* is to *grass* as *frog* is to _____.

3. *Snake* is to *reptile* as *beetle* is to _____.

4. *Muskrat* is to *fur* as *swallow* is to _____.

Phonemic Awareness

Rhyming Words

Rhyming word activities were a natural choice for these particular texts, which are full of rich rhymes. Practice in rhyming can be done in a variety of ways, depending on the ability level of your students. If your children are working with rhyme at the phonological level, you could do some of the following activities:

1. Make up silly sentences that use rhyming words from the text. "A tadpole doesn't *giggle*, but it does *wiggle*. Muskrats *stack*, then eat a *snack*."

2. Generate rhymes from words in the text. They can be real or nonsense words for this activity. "Can you think of a word that rhymes with _____?"

Phonemic-Awareness Bingo

Most phonemic-awareness skills that your students are working on can be adapted to a bingo game format using your target words. Chapter 5 gives details for developing bingo games with your students. Here's how it works for the sample unit.

1. **Beginning Sound Bingo:** Have your students write one letter in each box of their game board. You may want to give them a list of letters or sounds to choose from, or you may leave it up to their choice. Use the words from the texts, being sure to include your target vocabulary. Be sure to include a sentence that either defines the word or provides an example of how the word is used. For example:

   muskrat—"The *muskrat* is an animal that lives at the pond. If you have the letter you hear at the beginning of the word *muskrat*, you can cover that space."

   swoop—"The swallow will *swoop* down to get some food. If you have the letter you hear at the beginning of the word *swoop*, you can cover that space."

2. **Rhyming Word Bingo:** Provide students with a list of words from your master unit list that are easily rhymed. The students select eight words to write on their blank bingo cards. Use the following pattern to play the game.

   "If you have a word that rhymes with *giggle*, put a marker on its space." The student can then cover the space with the word *wiggle* from the text.

Cafeteria

Keep your word list in mind when you are in the cafeteria. Clearly some words will be easier to incorporate in this setting than others, but with a little creativity, you can find ways to include a few in the course of typical lunchroom exchanges.

- "You can *sip* your juice through the straw just like the *hummingbirds*."

- "You all sound like *caterpillars*—listen to all that *crunching* and *munching*!"

- "*Scurry* over and get some more napkins and we'll wipe up that spill."

- "When you dropped your milk, it *splattered* all over the floor."

Recess

If you are required to have organized activities during your recess time, or if you have to develop lessons for physical education, the following activities may be useful. They can be used anytime your students need an opportunity to burn off a little energy.

The active verbs from the Fleming texts are a natural for active games such as relay races. Divide your class into four teams—that keeps the wait time down for all concerned!

1. *Waddle* up to the line,
2. *circle* the cone, and
3. *scurry* back to the next child in line.

   or

1. *Hop* up to the line,
2. *twirl* a hula-hoop three times, and
3. *dart* back to the next child.

Math

Find ways to incorporate the vocabulary of the stories into your daily math instruction. The specific content objectives that you are working on will determine the best way for you to this. For example, for estimation and measurement concepts in math, vocabulary from the sample unit can be incorporated with the following kinds of questions:

- Which would be longer, a minnow or a muskrat?
- Which would weigh more, a tadpole or a frog?
- Which would move slower, the caterpillar or the ant?
- Which bird would have a wider wingspan, the swallow or the heron?

While working on addition and subtraction, word problems can feature the animals found in the text.

- There were five minnows swimming in the pond. A hungry heron ate two minnows. How many minnows were left in the pond?
- Three whirligigs were swirling and twirling in the pond. Two more came along and joined their fun. How many whirligigs in all?

To develop multiplication concepts for your math whiz kids, you might try more complex problems.

- How many wings would three dragonflies have?
- One turtle has four legs, so how many legs would two turtles have?

Science and Social Studies—If the Shoe Fits

Some lists of words will be a natural fit for infusion in your science and social studies lessons. Others will not match well, so don't force them. You'll have plenty of opportunities to use your target words in other parts of the day.

The texts we have been using for this unit would lend themselves well to a unit on habitats, food chains, or animals. You could sort the animals by mammal, reptile, bird, insect, or amphibian. Diagrams can be drawn showing the parts of the animals' bodies.

Music Connection

Many familiar children's songs can be adapted to match your theme and support the development of vocabulary through physical actions. These songs are most effective if you work with your children to develop the motions to go along with the words. The conversations that take place prove to be very powerful in developing understanding of the terms.

For example, you might start off by asking your children how the animals in the pond would show that they are happy in preparation for singing "If You're Happy and You Know It."

- "Do you think the geese would waddle if they were happy? Let's all try to waddle like the geese. What would that look like?"

You may sing the song several times during the two weeks of the unit. Select different animals from the pond (or grass) each time so it won't be too long. Ask the children to recall animals to sing about in the next verse.

- "What other animals can we sing about? What do they do?"

- "Can everyone picture what the heron looks like when it plunges its beak into the water?"

Questions of this type require the students to retrieve words from their semantic lexicon and to make the connections between the animal and its movement.

1. **"If You're Happy and You Know It—Pond Style"**
   This favorite children's song can be adapted to reflect the vocabulary of the stories. If you're happy and you know it:

   - *Waddle* like a goose (*arms folded like wings, waddle*)

   - *Wiggle* like a tadpole (*wiggle body or hand*)

   - *Lunge* like heron (*lunge down*)

   - *Swoop* like a bat (*using hand and arm to simulate swooping motion*)

   - *Scratch* like a mole (*scratch at the air*)

- *Glide* like a snake (*make gliding motion with hand and arm*)

- *Hop* like a rabbit (*hop up and down*)

2. **"If You're Happy and You Know It—Grass Style"**
   Change the words and the motions and you have a whole new song!

   - *Munch* like a caterpillar (*pretend to chew*)

   - *Sip* like a hummingbird (*pretend to sip as through a straw*)

   - *Hum* like a bee (*make a buzzing noise*)

   - *Flap* like a bird (*flap arms like wings*)

   - *Tug* like an ant (*pretend to pull a heavy object*)

   - *Glide* like a snake (*use arm to make a gliding motion*)

   - *Scratch* like a mole (*pretend to scratch the air or ground*)

   - *Scurry* like a beetle (*walk fingers quickly up arm*)

   - *Zap* like a frog (*quickly flick tongue in and out*)

   - *Hop* like a rabbit (*hop up and down*)

   - *Glow* like a firefly (*open and close hands on either side of face*)

   - *Swoop* like a bat (*use hand to make a swooping motion*)

3. **"The Critters in the Pond"**
   Use the familiar tune "The Wheels on the Bus" and adapt the text of the books to create a new song (with appropriate motions, of course).

   - The herons in the pond go *lunge* and *plunge.* (*make a lunging motion with legs, hold one arm and hand like the heron's neck and make a sharp downward motion on* plunge)

   - The tadpoles in the pond go *wiggle, jiggle, wriggle.* (*make wiggling motions either with the hand or whole body*)

   - The geese in the pond go *waddle, waddle, waddle.* (*waddle in place*)

   - The dragonflies in the pond, *hover* around. (*using hand as the dragonfly, make quick shaking motion, staying in place*)

   - The turtles in the pond, *drowse* and *doze.* (*head down on hands like sleeping*)

   - The minnows in the pond, *scatter, scatter, scatter.* (*quick hand motions in various directions*)

   - The whirligigs in the pond, *swirl* and *twirl.* (*turn around quickly in place*)

- The swallows in the pond, *swoop* and *scoop*. (*using the hand as the swallow, make swooping motion, with a downward swoop for scoop*)

- The crawfish in the pond, *click* and *clack*. (*simulate claws with hands*)

- The ducks in the pond, *dip* and *flip*. (*using hand, downward motion on dip, followed by turning over the hand on flip*)

- The raccoons in the pond, *splish* and *splash*. (*simulate raccoon washing his food in the water*)

- The muskrats in the pond, *pile* and *stack*. (*simulate piling sticks into a stack*)

4. **"The Critters in the Grass"**
   Use the "Wheels on the Bus" tune again, but adapt in to match the vocabulary of the *Tall, Tall Grass*.

   - The caterpillars in the grass, *crunch* and *munch*. (*inch finger up arm, pinching thumb and forefinger on crunch and munch*)

   - The hummingbirds in the grass, *dart, dip, sip*. (*make quick motions with hand for dart and dip, then suck in quickly after sip*)

   - The bees in the grass, *strum* and *hum*. (*make buzzing noise*)

   - The birds in the grass, *flap* their wings. (*flap arms like wings*)

   - The ants in the grass, *tug* and *lug*. (*simulate pulling a heavy object*)

   - The snakes in the grass, *slide* and *glide*. (*make a snake motion with your arm*)

   - The moles in the grass, *ritch, ratch, scratch*. (*simulate scratching at the ground*)

   - The beetles in the grass, *scurry* and *hurry*. (*move fingers quickly along arm*)

   - The frogs in the grass, *zip* and *zap*. (*quickly stick out tongue*)

   - The rabbits in the grass, *hip, hop, flop*. (*hold hands up like rabbit ears, hop twice, then on the word* flop, *flip your hands down*)

   - The fireflies in the grass, *glow* and *glow*. (*open and close hands*)

   - The bats in the grass, *loop* and *swoop*. (*make looping and swooping motion*)

You can allow students to select different verses to sing on different days, but you will want to be sure that you sing the verses with your target vocabulary words most frequently.

Conclusion

My hope is that this will not just be one more book on your shelf. My hope is that vocabulary will be infused into your life and into the lives of your students.

Take the ideas I have shared with you and mold them to meet the needs of your students. Shape the activities to match your unique personality and style. Give your creativity and imagination free reign and you will be amazed at the places you can find to infuse vocabulary.

Activities Chart

Most of the activities presented in this book can be used in a variety of contexts. This chart has been provided for you as a ready reference.

Activity (Page)	Oral Language	Writing	Math	Science	Social Studies	Centers
Act It Out (61)	✻				✻	
Analogies (36, 97)	✻		✻	✻	✻	
Bag Game (65)	✻					✻
Bingo (66)	✻					
Brainstorming (37, 71)	✻	✻		✻	✻	
Build a Cowboy (25)	✻			✻	✻	✻
Categories (35)	✻		✻	✻	✻	
Clothesline (80)			✻	✻	✻	✻
Crayon Activities (23)	✻	✻				✻
Concept Circles (79)			✻	✻	✻	✻
Daily Word(29)	✻	✻	✻	✻	✻	
Hangman (21)			✻	✻	✻	✻
Hink Pinks (20)	✻	✻				✻
I Spy (66)	✻					
Keyword Connections (24)			✻	✻	✻	✻
Line It Up (59, 85)			✻	✻	✻	✻
Linking Letters (84)			✻	✻	✻	
Making Words (67)	✻	✻				
Masterpiece Theater (48)	✻					✻
Mystery Bags (26)	✻					✻
Picture It (61)	✻	✻				
Picture This (24)	✻			✻	✻	✻
Sentence Hangman (21)	✻	✻				✻
Synonyms & Antonyms (37)	✻	✻				
Triple Plays (37, 76, 119)	✻	✻	✻	✻	✻	✻
Vocabulary 5 Ws (86)	✻	✻	✻	✻	✻	✻
Word Trees (83)			✻	✻	✻	✻

Alphabet Lists

Use these alphabet lists to get you started. My lists are in no way intended to be exhaustive, merely to provide a ready resource as you begin to try out infusion activities.

Some of the words will be quite familiar to your students. Think of new ways to incorporate them into your routines to expand the children's understanding. Other words will be quite new and will need explanations and repeated exposure in order to sink in.

Look at the curriculum for your school or district and add the words that appear in your content areas. Keep in mind that some words are used in a variety of ways. For example, once your children know *patriotic*, they can handle derivatives such as *patriotism*. When learning the word *justice* in social studies, create a Word Tree to help them see the connections to *judge, judicial,* and *judiciary*.

Alphabet books on a wide variety of themes are available in bookstores and libraries. These books, such as the series by Jerry Pallotta, can be a time-saving source of words— especially for the hard-to-find letters!

Create your own lists of words to meet the needs of your students. You may have children who are enthusiastic about insects or dinosaurs. Enlist the aid of your art and music teachers to start lists for those specialized subjects. Words that describe sounds or feelings are fun to create and provide a valuable resource for the students' writing.

Keep a list of words that are just fun to say, such as *caboodle, catastrophe, fiasco,* and *onomatopoeia*. Create the lists with your students' help. They will be more interested and excited about the words if they help collect them.

Texas

In my home state of Texas, we are all quite proud of the Lone Star State. Texas is an important part of the social studies curriculum from kindergarten on up to high school. Steven Kellogg's *Pecos Bill* (1986) is a fun tall tale to use to build some background knowledge for those of you from the rest of the states! This book features some great words: *ornery, coyote, ambush, varmint, trample,* and *hullabaloo!*

A — armadillo, Alamo
B — bluebonnet, bandana, bull, bronco
C — cowboy, cactus, corral, cattle
D — Dallas
E — expansive
F — flag
G — gulf
H — Houston, hurricane, horse, hay, herd
I — Indian paintbrush
J — jackrabbit
K — kin
L — longhorn, lariat, lasso, livestock, lone star
M — mockingbird, maverick
N — NASA
O — oil
P — pecan, prairie
Q — quail
R — range, rodeo, rattlesnake, reins
S — saddle, stampede, spurs
T — tornado
U — umbrella
V — valley
W — wagon
X — Texas
Y — yee haw
Z

Math

A — add, addend, addition, abacus, arc, angle

B — billion, base

C — calculate, calculator, calendar, circle, cylinder, compare, cone, coin

D — divide, dime, digit, difference, denominator, dollar

E — equal, equivalent, even, estimate

F — fact, factor, foot, fraction

G — gallon, greater, graph

H — half, hundred, hexagon, hour

I — increase, inch

J — join

K — kilo

L — less, length, liter

M — multiply, meter, minute

N — nickel, numeral, numerator

O — odd, octagon, one

P — pint, prism, penny, pentagon, polygon, pyramid, percent, parallel

Q — quart, quarter

R — radius, rectangle, rhombus

S — subtraction, square, sum, second

T — triangle, ten, thousand

U — unequal, unit

V — value, vertex, vertical, volume

W — weight, width

X — X coordinate

Y — yard

Z — zero

Science

A — accumulate, accelerate, absorb, adapt, atmosphere, amphibian

B — beaker, balance scale, brain

C — condensation, cycle, conservation, calcium, cell, Celsius, centigrade, chrysalis, climate, cloud

D — describe, diagram, dinosaur, discover

E — evaporation, energy, environment, erosion

F — force, fossil

G — galaxy, gravity, gas, germinate, germ

H — habitat, hand lens, hearing, hypothesis

I — investigation, insect

J — Jupiter, jet stream

K — kernel

L — larva, lava, liquid, lunar

M — mass, mammal, magma, magnet, matter, meteor, microscope

N — nerve, nocturnal

O — observation, orbit, organism, ozone

P — pattern, process, planet, plants, precipitation

Q — quantity

R — radar, rocks, roots, reptile

S — system, structure, safety, senses, sight, smell, soil, solid

T — temperature, taste, touch, thermometer

U — ultraviolet

V — Venus, vapor, vitamin, virus, volcano

W — water, weather, wind

X — X-ray

Y —

Z — zenith

Social Studies

A — America, allegiance, agriculture, Antarctica, Asia, Africa

B — ballot

C — custom, citizen, country, celebrate, canal, colony, capitol, century

D — democracy

E — eagle, equality, elect, Europe, equator, emblem

F — freedom, flag

G — governor, goods, globe

H — holiday

I — inventiveness, independence, international, island

J — justice, jobs

K — kayak

L — liberty, landforms, legislature

M — mayor

N — needs, nation, natural resource

O — obelisk, Oval Office

P — patriotic, president, pledge, peace

Q — quorum

R — rebel, recycle, rules, representative

S — services, symbols, Statue of Liberty, senator

T — truth, tax

U — unfair, unite

V — volunteer, vote

W — wants, White House, Washington

X

Y — Yankee

Z

Animals

After reading *Wild About Books* by Judy Sierra, your students will be ready to make their own animal alphabet books.

A — aardvark, anteater, alligator, anaconda, antelope, armadillo

B — baboon, bandicoot, boa constrictor, bear, beaver, badger, bat, bear, buffalo, bison

C — camel, caribou, cheetah, cougar, chinchilla, crocodile

D — dolphin

E — eagle, elephant, elk, ermine

F — fawn, fox

G — gull, giraffe, gecko, gorilla, gazelle, gnu, gerbil, goat

H — hamster, hyena, hippo, hedgehog

I — ibex

J — jaguar, javelina, jellyfish

K — kangaroo, koala

L — lion, llama, lynx, lemur, leopard

M — minnow, mink, moose, mongoose, monkey, muskrat, manatee

N — narwhal

O — octopus, otter, ocelot, opossum, orangutan

P — puma, python, panda, porcupine, platypus

Q — quarter horse, quail

R — rabbit, raccoon, rhinoceros

S — scorpion, squid, skink, stork, squirrel, seal, sloth, skunk

T — tarantula, termite, Tasmanian devil, tortoise, turtle

U — unicorn

V — vicuna

W — wildebeest, warthog, walrus, wolf, wombat

X

Y — yak

Z — zebra

Colors

A — azure, aqua, aquamarine, apricot

B — beige, black, blue, brown

C — crimson, chestnut, cobalt, chartreuse

D — denim, dandelion

E — ebony, ecru, emerald

F — fuchsia

G — gray, gold

H — honey

I — indigo, ivory

J — jade

K — khaki, kelly green

L — lemon, lavender

M — mauve, magenta, melon, mahogany, mustard

N — navy

O — olive, ochre

P — puce, peach, plum

Q

R — raspberry, rose, ruby

S — salmon, saffron, sienna, scarlet, silver

T — teal, tan

U — umber

V — violet

W — walnut, white

X

Y — yellow

Z

Birds

A — auk, albatross

B — blue jay

C — cardinal, cassowary, crow, chickadee, cuckoo

D — dove, duck

E — eagle, emu, egret

F — falcon, flamingo, finch

G — gull, goose

H — heron, hummingbird

I — ibis

J — jay, junco

K — kiwi, kittiwake, kingfisher

L — lark, loon

M — macaw, mockingbird, magpie

N — nene

O — owl, ostrich, osprey

P — penguin, pelican, partridge

Q — quail

R — roadrunner

S — swallow

T — tern

U —

V — vulture

W — woodpecker, wren, whippoorwill

X

Y — yellow-throat

Z — zebra finch

Foods

A — avocado, apricot, apple, asparagus

B — brunch, bacon, bagel, banana, barbecue, broccoli, beans, beet

C — cantaloupe, cabbage, cauliflower, celery, cereal, cheese, cherry, coconut, cucumber

D — donut

E — éclair, egg roll

F — fajita, fig, flan, fricassee

G — garlic, grape, gravy, grits

H — hamburger, herb, honeydew

I — ice cream

J — jelly

K — key lime, kiwi, kebab

L — lemon, lime, lamb, lettuce, lobster

M — macaroni, macaroon, mango

N — nectarine

O — orange, olive, omelet, oyster

P — papaya, pickle, pineapple, pasta, pizza, pancake, pear, peanut, peas, plum, popcorn

Q — quince, quesadilla

R — raspberry, rice, radish

S — salsa, salad, shrimp

T — tuna, tamale, taco, turnip

U — ugli fruit

V — vanilla, veal

W — walnut, watermelon, wonton

X

Y — yam, yogurt

Z

Flowers and Plants

A — azalea, aster, amaryllis

B — blossom, bachelor's button, begonia, bamboo, bluebell, buttercup

C — crocus, chrysanthemum, cactus, camellia, chamomile

D — daffodil, delphinium, daisy, dahlia

E — evening primrose

F — fern, forsythia

G — geranium, gladiola

H — honeysuckle, hibiscus, hyacinth, hydrangea

I — iris, impatiens, ivy, Indian paintbrush

J — jasmine

K — kalanchoe

L — lily, lupine, lotus

M — marigold, mum, magnolia

N — narcissus

O — oxeye daisy, orchid

P — petunia, pansy, periwinkle

Q — Queen Anne's lace

R — rose

S — snapdragon

T — tulip

U

V — Venus flytrap

W — wood violet, wisteria

X

Y

Z — zinnia

Around the House

A — armoire, attic, apron

B — banister, blanket, bucket

C — carpet, couch, cabinet, ceiling, cupboard, chandelier, clock, closet, cradle, crib, curtains, chimney

D — den, drapes

E — étagère, entertainment center

F — family, fridge, faucet, fence, fireplace, floor, freezer, furniture

G — garage, gate

H — hallway, hanger, high chair

I — iron, ironing board

J — jamb

K — kitchen, key

L — lamp, laundry, lawn, ladle, linoleum

M — mirror

N — napkin

O — oven, ottoman

P — pantry, pictures, plastic, piano

Q — quilt

R — rag, range, recliner, ribbon, roof

S — sofa, screen, stove, soap, spatula, skillet

T — table, tools, tongs, telephone, television

U — umbrella, utensil

V — vacuum

W — wall

X

Y — yard, yarn

Z

Verbs

Many of the words listed in science, social studies, and math are great verbs to incorporate in other areas of your day. Ask your students to *estimate* how long it will take them to finish their story, or to see if they can *discover* the answer in the text. Exposure to content words in multiple contexts will further develop your students' word knowledge.

A — ambush, abandon, abate, ache, achieve, act, aggravate, announce, arrive

B — balance, beg, bombard, budget

C — carve, charge, chatter, chuckle, collect, classify, collide, comment, compliment

D — dawdle, doze, devour, declare, demolish

E — enter, eliminate, estimate

F — fidget, flip, force, forecast, frustrate

G — guide, glide, gather, giggle, glance, grasp

H — handle, hesitate, hover, huddle

I — inch, illustrate, imagine, imitate, inform, introduce

J — jiggle, juggle, jumble

K — kindle

L — label, lunge, lurk

M — maintain

N — nibble, notice

O — object

P — plunge, panic, pry, parade, participate, persist, persuade,

Q — quarrel

R — race, ramble, reflect

S — scatter, scamper, scold, scramble, snap

T — tally, twirl

U — unite

V — vacate, vanish, vary

W — wander

X

Y — yank, yield

Z — zoom

Thanksgiving—Fall

A — acorn

B — boat

C — cornucopia, cranberry

D — deer

E — England

F — freedom, feast

G — gourd

H — harvest

I — Indian

J — journey

K — kind, keel

L — leaves

M — meal, Mayflower

N — natives

O — ocean

P — pumpkin, Pilgrim, Plimoth

Q

R — rebel

S — succotash

T — turkey

U

V — venison

W — welcome, wampum

X

Y — yam

Z — zeal

Holidays

If you teach in a multicultural school, your students will be able to help you fill in this list. Creating an alphabet list is a great way to honor everyone's culture and to learn about customs and traditions from other countries.

A — anniversary
B — birthday
C — candles, cards, carols, cookies
D — decorations, dreidel
E — Easter, egg, elf
F — fireworks, fiesta
G — gifts, garland, groundhog
H — holly, hearts, Hanukkah
I — icicles
J — Jack Frost, jack o' lantern
K — Kwanzaa
L — leprechaun
M — mask, menorah, mistletoe
N — New Year
O — ornaments
P — pumpkins, parades, presents, piñata
Q
R — reindeer, rainbow, resolution, red envelopes
S — stockings, sleigh, shamrock
T — tinsel, turkey
U
V — valentines
W — wreath
X
Y — yule
Z

Triple Plays

The following lists of words can help you when you want to complete a Triple Play activity with your class. Triple Plays can be done in a whole-class format for younger students and developing readers and writers, or they can be completed independently for more fluent readers and writers. Additional examples and explanations can be found Chapter 6.

Provide your students with the word for the center of the Triple Play. Be sure to tell them whether you are looking for words with positive and negative connotations, or if you are looking for words that indicate a lesser or greater degree. Both kinds of examples are given in the following charts. The connotation sets come first, then the ones that vary by degree. Depending on your instructions, the order of the words may change from how they are presented here.

You may even find Triple Plays can help you, too! Experienced teachers know that selecting just the right word to express what you are trying to say to a parent is critical. If the word you select has a negative connotation, the parent sometimes reacts defensively. The same message may be expressed with a different word, one that will keep the lines of communication open.

Emotions

−		+
anxious	nervous	excited
pleased	thankful	grateful
happy	thrilled	ecstatic
upset	angry	furious
unhappy	sad	miserable
like	love	adore

Verbs

−		+
annoy	bother	pester
summon	hail	call
battle	quarrel	disagree
demolish	wreck	damage
hop	jump	leap
snip	cut	slash
direct	show	guide
tug	pull	drag
shout	yell	shriek

Adjectives

−		+
plain	usual	normal
defect	weakness	imperfection
big	large	immense
bony	thin	lean
weird	unusual	exotic
sluggish	slow	leisurely
shrewd	smart	brilliant
moist	damp	soggy
unsafe	risky	dangerous
filthy	unclean	dirty
laughable	funny	humorous
unkind	mean	cruel
exhausted	fatigued	tired
plain	homely	ugly
nice	pleasant	enjoyable
jagged	rough	uneven
necessary	essential	vital

Nouns

−		+
accident	disaster	catastrophe
war	fight	disagreement
agony	pain	hurt
enemy	opponent	challenger

Math

−		+
penny	nickel	dime
ones	tens	hundreds
second	minute	hour
day	week	month
inch	foot	yard
cup	pint	quart

Science

–		+
frigid	cold	cool
breeze	wind	gale
gloomy	overcast	cloudy
mist	drizzle	downpour
warm	hot	boiling

Social Studies

–		+
dictator	ruler	leader
pond	lake	ocean
pebble	rock	boulder
state	country	continent
mayor	governor	president
city	county	state

Helpful Hints

1. Develop your own vocabulary. Subscribe to an online Listserv that will provide you with a word of the day. Many are available free of charge, such as the Merriam-Webster Web site. (http://www.m-w.com).

2. Start a file with collections of words and ideas of your own. Every class is different, and each of you has a unique style. Use your own interests as well as those of your students as starting points.

3. Keep a record of the words you introduce and the context in which you used them. This will allow you to keep track of the words the children have been exposed to.

4. Encourage your students to become word collectors. Set aside time each day when they can share interesting words that they have heard at home. Discuss the meanings of the words and where they were heard. You may need to keep a dictionary handy for this—I always seemed to have at least one student who tried to come up with a word I didn't know! Display a class list of these words along with the name of the student who contributed them.

5. Reflect at the end of the day. Were there lost opportunities for developing vocabulary? Were there words that were introduced in a read-aloud that should be reviewed in a morning message or in some other context?

6. Anticipate tomorrow. While many of the best infusion moments are unplanned and spontaneous, you can and should plan for the more structured activities.

Children's Books

Arnosky, J. (1999). *All about owls*. New York: Scholastic.

Cooney, B. (1985). *Miss Rumphius*. New York: Puffin Books.

Dickinson, E. (1924). *The complete poems of Emily Dickinson*. Boston: Little, Brown.

Ehlert, L. (1994). *Eating the alphabet: Fruits and vegetables from A to Z*. New York: Harcourt

Ehlert, L. (1992). *Planting a rainbow*. New York: Voyager Books.

Ferraro, B. (2003). *Be a good citizen*. New York: Sadlier-Oxford.

Fleming, D. (1993). *In the small, small pond*. New York: Scholastic.

Fleming, D. (1995). *In the tall, tall grass*. New York: Holt.

Gwyne, F. (1976). *A chocolate moose for dinner*. New York: Simon & Schuster.

Gwyne, F. (1988). *The king who rained*. New York: Simon & Schuster.

Henkes, K. (1996). *Chrysanthemum*. New York: HarperCollins.

Hutchins, P. (1993). *The wind blew*. New York: Scholastic.

Kellogg, S. (1986). *Pecos Bill*. New York: Scholastic.

Pallotta, J. Alphabet book series. Watertown, MA: Charlesbridge.

Pasquarella, A. (2001). *The writer's thesaurus*, Level 1. Merrimack, NH: Options.

Pelham, D. (1989). *Worms wiggle*. New York: Simon & Schuster.

Sierra, J. (2006). *Wild about books*. New York: Knopf.

White, E. B. (1969). *Charlotte's web*. New York: Dell.

White, N. (2002). *The magic school bus explores the world of bugs*. New York: Scholastic.

Wise, W. (2004). *Ten sly piranhas: A counting story in reverse (A tale of wickedness—and worse!)*. New York: Puffin Books.

Yolen, J. (1993). *Welcome to the green house*. New York: Scholastic.

References

Baumann, J. F., Kame'enui, E. J., & Ash, G. E. (2003). Research on vocabulary instruction: Voltaire redux. In J. Flood, D. Lapp, J. R. Squire, & M. Jensen (Eds.), *Handbook on research on teaching the English language arts* (2nd ed., pp. 752–785). Mahwah, NJ: Erlbaum.

Beck, I. L., McKeown, M. G., & Kucan, L. (2002). *Bringing words to life: Robust vocabulary instruction*. New York: Guilford Press.

Beers, K. (2002). *When kids can't read: What teachers can do: A guide for teachers 6–12*. Portsmouth, NH: Heinemann.

Biemiller, A. (2003). Vocabulary: Needed if more children are to read well. *Reading Psychology, 24*, 323–335.

Biemiller, A. (2001). Teaching vocabulary: Early, direct, and sequential. *American Educator, 25*(1), 24–28.

Biemiller, A., & Boote, C. (2006). An effective method for building meaning vocabulary in primary grades. *Journal of Educational Psychology, 98*, 44–62.

Blachowicz, C. L., & Fisher, P. (2000). Vocabulary instruction. In M. Kamil, P. Mosentahl, P. D. Pearson, & R. Barr (Eds.), *Handbook of reading research: Volume III* (pp. 503–523), Mahwah, NJ: Erlbaum.

Buchoff, R. (1996). Riddles: Fun with language across the curriculum. *The Reading Teacher, 49*, 66–68.

Chall, J. S., & Snow, C. E. (1988). Influences on reading in low-income students. *The Education Digest, 54*(1), 53–56.

Cummins, J. (1983). Language proficiency, biliteracy, and French immersion. *Canadian Journal of Education, 8*(2), 117–138.

Cunningham, P. (2000). *Phonics they use*. New York: Longman.

Cunningham, P. M., Moore, S. A., Cunningham, J. W., & Moore, D. W. (2004). *Reading and writing in elementary classrooms: Research-based K–4 instruction*. New York: Longman.

Dale, E. (1965). Vocabulary measurement: Techniques and main findings. *Elementary English, 42*, 895-901.

Dickinson, D. K., & Tabors, P. O. (2001). *Beginning literacy with language: Young children learning at home and school.* Baltimore: Brookes.

Durso, F. T., & Coggins, K. A. (1991). Organized instruction for the improvement of word knowledge skills. *Journal of Educational Psychology, 83*, 108–112.

Genesee, F. (1985). Second language learning through immersion: A review of U.S. programs. *Review of Educational Research, 55*(4), 541-561.

Graves, M. F. (2006). *The vocabulary book: Learning and instruction.* New York: Teachers College Press.

Graves, M. F. (1986). Vocabulary learning and instruction. In E. Z. Rothkopf & L. C. Ehri (Eds.), *Review of research in education* (Vol. 13, pp. 48–89). Washington, DC: American Education Research Association.

Greenwood, S. C. (2002). Making words matter: Vocabulary study in the content areas. *The Clearing House, 75*(5), 258–263.

Hall, A. K. (1995). Sentencing: The psycholinguistic guessing game. *The Reading Teacher, 49*(1), 76–77.

Harmon, J. M., Wood, K. D., & Hedrick, W. B. (2006). *Instructional strategies for teaching content vocabulary.* Newark, DE: International Reading Association.

Hart, B., & Risley, R. T. (1995). *Meaningful differences in the everyday experience of young American children.* Baltimore: Brookes.

Hayes, D. P., & Ahrens, M. (1988). Vocabulary simplification for children: A special case of "motherese." *Journal of Child Language, 15*, 392–410.

Hirsch, E. D. (2005). Reading comprehension requires knowledge—of words and the world. In Z. Fang (Ed.), *Literacy teaching and learning: Current issues and trends* (pp. 121–132). Upper Saddle River, NJ: Pearson.

Hirsch, E. D. (2003). Reading comprehension requires knowledge: Of words and the world. *American Educator, 27*, 10–13.

Hoyt, L. (2005). Building a robust vocabulary. In L. Hoyt (Ed.), *Spotlight on comprehension* (pp. 161–173). Portsmouth, NH: Heinemann.

HuffBenkoski, K. A., & Greenwood, S. C. (1995). The use of word analogy with developing reading. *The Reading Teacher, 48*, 446–47.

Lewkowicz, N. (1994). The bag game: An activity to heighten phonemic awareness. *The Reading Teacher, 47*, 508–509.

MacIntyre, P. D., Baker, S. C., Clement, R., & Donovan, L. A. (2003). Willingness to communicate and intensive language programs. *Canadian Modern Language Review, 59*, 589–607.

McCormick, S. (2007). *Instructing students who have literacy problems* (5th ed.). Upper Saddle River, NJ: Pearson Prentice Hall.

McGee, L. M., & Richgels, D. J. (2003). Designing early literacy programs: Strategies for at-risk preschool and kindergarten children. New York: Guilford Press.

Metsala, J. L. (1999). Young children's phonological awareness and non-word repetition as a function of vocabulary development. *Journal of Educational Psychology, 91*, 3–19.

Metsala, J., & Walley, A. (1998). Spoken vocabulary growth and the segmental restructuring of lexical representations: Precursors to phonemic awareness and early reading ability. In J. Metsala & L. Ehri (Eds.), *Word recognition in beginning literacy* (pp. 89–120). Mahwah, NJ: Erlbaum.

Morrow, L. M. (1997). *Literacy development in the early years: Helping children read and write.* Boston: Allyn & Bacon.

Mountain, L. H. (2000). *Early 3Rs: How to lead beginners into reading, writing, and arithme-talk.* Mahwah, NJ: Erlbaum.

Nagy, W. E., & Scott, J. A. (2000). Vocabulary processes. In M. Kamil, P. Mosentahl, P. D. Pearson, & R. Barr (Eds.), *Handbook of reading research: Volume III* (pp. 269–284), Mahwah, NJ: Erlbaum.

National Reading Panel. (2000). *Teaching children to read: An evidence based assessment of the scientific research literature on reading and its implications for reading instruction.* Washington, DC: National Institute of Child Health and Human Development.

Nation, K., & Snowling, M. J. (2004). Beyond phonological skills: Broader language skills contribute to the development of reading. *Journal of Research in Reading, 72*(4), 342–356.

Owens, R. E. (2001). *Language development: An introduction.* Boston: Allyn & Bacon.

Rickards, D., & Hawes, S. (2007). Connecting reading and writing through author's craft. *The Reading Teacher, 60*, 370–373.

Stead, T. (2006, November). Keynote address. Texas State Reading Association 35th Annual State Literacy Conference, Austin, TX.

Tompkins, G. E. (2006). *Literacy for the 21st century: Teaching reading and writing in prekindergarten through grade 4.* Upper Saddle River, NJ: Pearson.

White, T. G., Graves, M. F., & Slater, W. H. (1990). Growth of reading vocabulary in diverse elementary schools: Decoding and word meaning. *Journal of Educational Psychology, 82*, 281–290.